ENVIRONMENTAL REMEDIATION TECHNOLOGIES, REGULATIONS AND SAFETY

ELECTRONIC WASTE

REUSE, RECYCLING AND EXPORT CONSIDERATIONS

ENVIRONMENTAL REMEDIATION TECHNOLOGIES, REGULATIONS AND SAFETY

Additional books in this series can be found on Nova's website under the Series tab.

Additional E-books in this series can be found on Nova's website under the E-book tab.

WASTE AND WASTE MANAGEMENT

Additional books in this series can be found on Nova's website under the Series tab.

Additional E-books in this series can be found on Nova's website under the E-book tab.

ENVIRONMENTAL REMEDIATION TECHNOLOGIES, REGULATIONS AND SAFETY

ELECTRONIC WASTE

REUSE, RECYCLING AND EXPORT CONSIDERATIONS

JERMAINE L. PRICE
AND
RICHARD C. COOPER
EDITORS

Nova Science Publishers, Inc.
New York

For permission to use material from this book please contact us:
Telephone 631-231-7269; Fax 631-231-8175
Web Site: http://www.novapublishers.com

Library of Congress Cataloging-in-Publication Data

ISBN: 978-1-62081-617-2

Published by Nova Science Publishers, Inc. † New York

CONTENTS

PREFACE

Each year, consumers purchase millions of electronic devices, such as televisions, computers, and cell phones, and are faced with what to do with their used electronics. Recycling can recover a variety of materials, including precious metals, and many electronics can be reused or contain reusable components. Yet, the Environmental Protection Agency (EPA) and industry data show that tens of millions of used electronics are thrown away each year. Moreover, because used electronics often contain toxic substances, such as lead and mercury, their end-of-life management raises concerns about the potential adverse impacts on human health and the environment, particularly when used electronics are exported to countries that lack a safe recycling and disposal capacity. This book examines the EPA's current efforts to facilitate the environmentally sound management of used electronics, with a focus on the view of manufacturers, retailers, recyclers, state and local governments, and other stakeholders.

Chapter 1 - Low recycling rates for used televisions, computers, and other electronics result in the loss of valuable resources, and electronic waste exports risk harming human health and the environment in countries that lack safe recycling and disposal capacity. The Environmental Protection Agency (EPA) regulates the management of used electronics that qualify as hazardous waste and promotes voluntary efforts among electronics manufacturers, recyclers, and other stakeholders. However, in the absence of a comprehensive national approach, a growing number of states have enacted electronics recycling laws, raising concerns about a patchwork of state requirements. In this context, GAO examined (1) EPA's efforts to facilitate environmentally sound used electronics management, (2) the views of various stakeholders on the state-by-state approach, and (3) considerations to further promote environmentally sound management. GAO reviewed EPA documents, interviewed EPA officials, and interviewed stakeholders in five states with electronics recycling legislation.

Chapter 2 - Electronic waste (e-waste) is a term that is used loosely to refer to obsolete, broken, or irreparable electronic devices like televisions, computer central processing units (CPUs), computer monitors (flat screen and cathode ray tubes), laptops, printers, scanners, and associated wiring. E-waste has become a concern in the United States due to the high volumes in which it is generated, the hazardous constituents it often contains (such as lead, mercury, and chromium), and the lack of regulations applicable to its disposal or recycling.

Under most circumstances, e-waste can legally be disposed of in a municipal solid waste landfill or recycled with few environmental regulatory requirements. Concerns about e-waste landfill disposal have led federal and state environmental agencies to encourage recycling. To date, 23 states have enacted some form of mandatory e-waste recycling program. These state requirements, mixed with increased consumer awareness regarding potential problems with landfilling e-waste, have led to an increase in recycling. With that increase have come new questions about e-waste management. Instead of questions only about the potential impacts associated with e-waste *disposal*, questions have arisen regarding the potential danger associated with e-waste *recycling*—particularly when recycling involves the export of e-waste to developing countries where there are few requirements to protect workers or the environment.

Answering questions about both e-waste disposal and recycling involves a host of challenges. For example, little information is available to allow a complete assessment of how e-waste is ultimately managed. General estimates have been made about the management of cathode ray tubes (CRTs, the only devices where disposal is federally regulated), but little reliable information is available regarding other categories of e-waste. For example, accurate data regarding how much is generated, how it is managed (through disposal or recycling), and where it is processed (domestically or abroad) are largely unknown. Further, little information is available regarding the total amount of functioning electronics exported to developing countries for legitimate reuse.

What *is* known is that e-waste recycling involves complex processes and it is more costly to recycle e-waste in the United States. It also is known that most consumer electronics manufacturers (who provide the market for material recovery from recycled electronics) have moved overseas. As a result, the majority of e-waste collected for recycling (either for reuse or recycling) appears to be exported for processing.

Although there may be limited data regarding how e-waste is managed, the consequences of export to developing countries that manage it improperly are becoming increasingly evident. In particular, various reports and studies (by the mainstream media, environmental organizations, and university researchers) have found primitive waste management practices in India and various countries in Africa and Asia. Operations in Guiyu in the Shantou region of China have gained particular attention. Observed recycling operations involve burning the plastic coverings of materials to extract metals for scrap, openly burning circuit boards to remove solder or soaking them in acid baths to strip them for gold or other metals. Acid baths are then dumped into surface water. Among other impacts to those areas have been elevated blood lead levels in children and soil and water contaminated with heavy metals.

The impacts associated with e-waste exports have led to concerns from environmental organizations, members of the public, and some Members of Congress.

Chapter 3 - Electronic waste (e-waste) is a term that loosely refers to obsolete, broken, or irreparable electronic devices like televisions, computer central processing units (CPUs), computer monitors, laptops, printers, scanners, and associated wiring. Because e-waste is generated in high volumes in the United States and contains hazardous materials like lead, mercury, and chromium, it is a growing area of domestic concern. Currently, e-waste is essentially unregulated at the federal level and can be disposed of with common household garbage in municipal solid waste landfills or incinerators. However, the international trade in e-waste is subject to the international agreements governing the hazardous waste trade. The United States is a party to several of these agreements, but it is not a party to the largest multilateral agreement in this field: the Basel Convention.

Although it is difficult to know exactly how much e-waste is exported from the United States, developing countries in Asia or Africa appear to be active importers of it. Many of these countries lack, or do not enforce, labor or environmental laws that would mitigate or prevent the harms to human and environmental health that are associated with e-waste processing. The result is that some overseas e-waste recycling operations may pose a significant risk to human and environmental well-being.

Recently, momentum has developed for domestic legislation restricting U.S. e-waste exports. These restrictions could take many forms, including a partial or total ban on e-waste exports, an e-waste export licensing system, or a quota on e-waste exports. However, these restrictions may be difficult to reconcile with the General Agreement on Tariffs and Trade (GATT), one of the World Trade Organization (WTO) Agreements, and could be susceptible to challenge before a WTO panel.

In particular, e-waste export restrictions may be deemed inconsistent with Articles XI:1, XIII:1, and I:1 of the GATT. If declared a violation of the GATT, e-waste export restrictions could be justified under Article XX of the GATT if they (1) fit under one of the exceptions listed in paragraphs (a) to (j) of Article XX of the GATT and (2) satisfy the requirements imposed by the Article XX chapeau. It would be difficult, however, for U.S. export restrictions on e-waste to meet this standard for justification if they are imposed without serious U.S. engagement in international negotiations on the hazardous waste trade or without the concurrent operation of comparable restrictions on domestic e-waste production.

In: Electronic Waste
Editors: J. L. Price and R. C. Cooper

ISBN 978-1-62081-617-2

Chapter 1

ELECTRONIC WASTE: CONSIDERATIONS FOR PROMOTING ENVIRONMENTALLY SOUND REUSE AND RECYCLING*

The United States Government Accountability Office

WHY GAO DID THIS STUDY

Low recycling rates for used televisions, computers, and other electronics result in the loss of valuable resources, and electronic waste exports risk harming human health and the environment in countries that lack safe recycling and disposal capacity. The Environmental Protection Agency (EPA) regulates the management of used electronics that qualify as hazardous waste and promotes voluntary efforts among electronics manufacturers, recyclers, and other stakeholders. However, in the absence of a comprehensive national approach, a growing number of states have enacted electronics recycling laws, raising concerns about a patchwork of state requirements. In this context, GAO examined (1) EPA's efforts to facilitate environmentally sound used electronics management, (2) the views of various stakeholders on the state-by-state approach, and (3) considerations to further promote environmentally sound management. GAO reviewed EPA documents, interviewed EPA

* This is an edited, reformatted and augmented version of The United States Government Accountability Office publication, Report to the Chairman, Committee on Science and Technology, House of Representatives GAO-10-626, dated July 2010.

officials, and interviewed stakeholders in five states with electronics recycling legislation.

WHAT GAO RECOMMENDS

GAO recommends that the Administrator, EPA, (1) examine how EPA's partnership programs could be improved to contribute more effectively to used electronics management and (2) work with other federal agencies to finalize a legislative proposal on ratification of the Basel Convention for congressional consideration. EPA agreed with the recommendations.

WHAT GAO FOUND

EPA's efforts to facilitate the environmentally sound management of used electronics consist largely of (1) enforcing its rule for the recycling and exporting of cathode-ray tubes (CRT), which contain significant quantities of lead, and (2) an array of partnership programs that encourage voluntary efforts among manufacturers and other stakeholders. EPA has improved enforcement of export provisions of its CRT rule, but issues related to exports remain. In particular, EPA does not specifically regulate the export of many other electronic devices, such as cell phones, which typically are not within the regulatory definition of hazardous waste despite containing some toxic substances. In addition, the impact of EPA's partnership programs is limited or uncertain, and EPA has not systematically analyzed the programs to determine how their impact could be augmented. The views of stakeholders on the state-by-state approach to managing used electronics have been shaped by the increasing number of states with electronics recycling legislation. To varying degrees, the entities typically regulated under the state laws—electronics manufacturers, retailers, and recyclers—consider the increasing number of state laws to be a compliance burden. In contrast, in the five states GAO visited, state and local solid waste management officials expressed overall support for states taking a lead role in the absence of a national approach. The officials attributed their varying levels of satisfaction more to the design and implementation of individual state recycling programs, rather than to the state-by-state approach. Options to further promote the environmentally sound management of used electronics involve a number of policy considerations and encompass many variations, which generally range from a continued reliance on state recycling programs to the establishment of federal standards via legislation. The first approach provides the greatest degree of flexibility to states but does not address stakeholder concerns that the state-by-state approach is a compliance burden or will leave some states without electronics recycling programs. Moreover, EPA does not have a plan for coordinating its efforts with state recycling programs or articulating how EPA's partnership programs can best assist stakeholders to achieve the environmentally sound management of used electronics. Under the second approach, a primary policy issue is the degree to which federal standards would allow for stricter state standards, thereby providing states with flexibility but also potentially worsening the compliance burden from the standpoint of regulated entities. As a component of any approach, a greater federal regulatory role over exports could address limitations on the authority of states to regulate exports. GAO previously recommended that EPA submit to Congress a legislative proposal for ratification of the Basel Convention, a multilateral environmental agreement that aims to protect against the adverse effects resulting from transboundary movements of hazardous waste. EPA officials told GAO that the agency had developed a legislative proposal under previous administrations but had not finalized a proposal with other federal agencies.

ABBREVIATIONS

CalRecycle	Department of Resources Recycling and Recovery
CRT	cathode-ray tube
EPA	Environmental Protection Agency
EPEAT	Electronic Product Environmental Assessment Tool
R2	Responsible Recycling

July 12, 2010
The Honorable Bart Gordon
Chairman
Committee on Science and Technology House of Representatives

Dear Mr. Chairman:

Each year, consumers purchase millions of electronic devices, such as televisions, computers, and cell phones, and are faced with what to do with their used electronics. Recycling[1] can recover a variety of materials, including precious metals, and many electronics can be reused or contain reusable components. Yet, Environmental Protection Agency (EPA) and industry data show that tens of millions of used electronics are thrown away each year. Moreover, because used electronics often contain toxic substances, such as lead and mercury, their end-of-life management raises concerns about the potential adverse impacts on human health and the environment, particularly when used electronics are exported to countries that lack a safe recycling and disposal capacity.

The management of used electronics may be subject to a combination of federal and state regulations as well as nonregulatory, or voluntary, efforts. At the federal level, EPA regulates the handling and disposal of used electronics that qualify as hazardous waste, such as those that fail EPA's tests for toxicity.[2] In particular, items with cathode-ray tubes (CRT), such as older televisions and computer monitors, contain significant quantities of lead. EPA also works with electronics manufacturers, retailers, and recyclers; state governments; environmental groups; and other stakeholders under partnership programs that seek to ensure the environmentally sound management of used electronics.

At the state level, numerous states have enacted laws establishing electronics collection and recycling programs, including mechanisms for funding the cost of recycling. As of June 2010, 23 states had enacted some type of electronics recycling legislation. Other states have banned certain electronics from landfills or funded voluntary recycling efforts. Such efforts have increased recycling opportunities for consumers but raised concerns about the growth of a patchwork of state requirements.

In this context, GAO examined (1) EPA's current efforts to facilitate the environmentally sound management of used electronics; (2) the views of manufacturers, retailers, recyclers, state and local governments, and other stakeholders on the current state-by-state approach to the management of used electronics; and (3) considerations for further promoting the environmentally sound management of used electronics.

To address these objectives, we reviewed EPA documents and interviewed EPA officials regarding efforts to promote the environmentally sound management of used electronics. We also interviewed representatives of an array of national organizations of stakeholders affected by or concerned with management of used electronics, including manufacturers, retailers, recyclers, state and local governments, and environmental groups. To gain insights into the impact of state electronics recycling laws, we studied in detail the programs in five states—California, Maine, Minnesota, Texas, and Washington. We selected states to represent a range of models for financing recycling programs.

In addition, we selected states with recycling programs that had been in place long enough for stakeholders to provide an assessment of the impacts of the legislation.

In each state, we interviewed representatives of state and local governments, collectors and recyclers of used electronics that operate under the state program as well as refurbishers of used electronics, state retail associations, and state environmental groups. During these interviews, we generally discussed the impact of state legislation on collection rates for used electronics, convenience of disposal options for consumers, and environmentally sound management of electronics collected under the state programs.

We also obtained stakeholders' views on options to further promote the environmentally sound management of used electronics. While recognizing that stakeholders may benefit from state legislation, such as through an increase in business opportunities for electronics recyclers, we specifically asked about the burden (if any) created by the state-by-state approach.

We encountered a number of limitations in the availability of reliable data on the impact of the state-by-state approach on various stakeholders. For example, the five states we selected did not have data on collection and recycling rates prior to the effective dates of their laws, which would be useful to quantify the impact of their programs.

Similarly, some manufacturers and other stakeholders regulated under state laws had concerns about providing us with proprietary information or did not identify compliance costs in a way that enabled us to determine the portion of costs that stems from having to comply with differing state requirements. Due to such limitations, we relied predominately on stakeholders' statements regarding how they have been impacted under the state-by-state approach. Appendix I contains detailed information on the scope and methodology of this report.

We conducted this performance audit from May 2009 to July 2010 in accordance with generally accepted government auditing standards. Those standards require that we plan and perform the audit to obtain sufficient, appropriate evidence to provide a reasonable basis for our findings and conclusions based on our audit objectives. We believe that the evidence obtained provides a reasonable basis for our findings and conclusions based on our audit objectives.

BACKGROUND

The management of used electronics presents a number of environmental and health concerns. EPA estimates that only 15 to 20 percent of used electronics (by weight) are collected for reuse and recycling, and that the remainder of collected materials is primarily sent to U.S. landfills. While a survey conducted by the consumer electronics industry suggests that EPA's data may underestimate the recycling rate, the industry survey confirms that the number of used electronics thrown away each year is in the tens of millions. As a result, valuable resources contained in electronics, including copper, gold, and aluminum, are lost for future use. Additionally, while modern landfills are designed to prevent leaking of toxic substances and contamination of groundwater, research shows that some types of electronics have the potential to leach toxic substances with known adverse health effects. Used electronics may also be exported for recycling or disposal. In August 2008, we reported that, while such exports can be handled responsibly in countries with effective regulatory regimes and by companies with advanced technologies, a substantial amount ends up in countries that lack the capacity to safely recycle and dispose of used electronics.[3]

We also have previously reported on the economic and other factors that inhibit recycling and reuse.[4] For example, many recyclers charge fees because their costs exceed the revenue they receive from selling recycled commodities or refurbishing units. Household electronics, in particular, are typically older and more difficult to refurbish and resell, and, thus, may have less value than those from large institutions. In most states, it is easier and cheaper for consumers to dispose of household electronics at a local landfill. Moreover, as EPA and others have noted, the domestic infrastructure to recycle used electronics is limited, and the major markets for both recycled commodities and reusable equipment are overseas.

The United States does not have a comprehensive national approach for the reuse and recycling of used electronics, and previous efforts to establish a national approach have been unsuccessful. Under the National Electronics Product Stewardship Initiative, a key previous effort that was initially funded by EPA, stakeholders met between 2001 and 2004, in part to develop a financing system to facilitate reuse and recycling. Stakeholders included representatives of federal, state, and local governments; electronics manufacturers, retailers, and recyclers; and environmental organizations. Yet despite broad agreement in principle, stakeholders in the process did not reach agreement on a uniform, nationwide financing system. For example, they did not reach agreement on a uniform system that would address the unique issues related to televisions, which have longer life spans and cost more to recycle than computers. In the absence of a national approach, some states have since addressed the management of used electronics through legislation or other means, and other stakeholders are engaged in a variety of voluntary efforts.

State Electronics Recycling Legislation

In the 9 years that have passed since stakeholders initiated the National Electronics Product Stewardship Initiative in an ultimately unsuccessful attempt to develop a national financing system to facilitate the reuse and recycling of used electronics, 23 states have enacted some form of electronics recycling legislation. For example, some of these state laws established an electronics collection and recycling program and a mechanism for funding the cost of recycling (see fig. 1).

Sources: GAO analysis of state electronics recycling laws; Map Resources (map).

Figure 1. States with Electronics Recycling Legislation.

The state laws represent a range of options for financing the cost of recycling and also differ in other respects, such as the scope of electronic devices covered under the recycling programs, with televisions, laptop computers, and computer monitors frequently among the covered electronic devices.[5] Similarly, while the state laws generally cover used electronics generated by households, some laws also cover used electronics generated by small businesses, charities, and other entities.

Five of the states—California, Maine, Minnesota, Texas, and Washington— represent some of the key differences in financing mechanisms. California was early to enact legislation and is the only state to require that electronics retailers collect a recycling fee from consumers at the time of purchase of a new electronic product covered under the law. These fees are deposited into a fund managed by the state and used to pay for the collection and recycling of used electronics.

In contrast, the other four states have enacted legislation making manufacturers selling products in their jurisdictions responsible for recycling or for some or all of the recycling costs. Such laws are based on the concept of "producer responsibility" but implement the concept in different ways. In Maine, state-approved consolidators of covered used electronics bill individual manufacturers, with the amount billed for particular electronics being based in part either on the manufacturer's market share of products sold or on the share of used electronics collected under the state's program. Under the Minnesota law, manufacturers either must meet recycling targets by arranging and paying for the collection and recycling of an amount in weight based on a percentage of their sales or must pay recycling fees. Texas requires that manufacturers establish convenient "take-back" programs for their own brands of equipment. Finally, the Washington law requires that manufacturers establish and fund collection services that meet certain criteria for convenience, as well as transportation and recycling services. Table 1 summarizes the key characteristics of the electronics recycling legislation in these five states.

Other State and Voluntary Efforts

As of June 2010, the remaining 27 states had not enacted legislation to establish electronics recycling programs. In some of these states, legislation concerning electronics recycling has been proposed, and some state legislatures have established commissions to study options for the management of used electronics.

Table 1. Key Characteristics of the Electronics Recycling Legislation in Five Selected States

State	Program start date	Financing mechanism	Covered electronic devices	Entities whose discarded devices are covered
California	2005	Retailers collect a fee from consumers at the point of sale. The state uses the fees to pay for collection and recycling.	Video display devices with a screen size greater than 4 inches, measured diagonally, identified in regulations as presumed hazardous	Any user of a covered electronic device located within the state
Maine	2006	Municipalities provide collection and arrange transport to state-approved consolidators, which generally bill individual manufacturers for recycling costs.	Computers, printers, video game consoles, and video display devices with a screen size greater than 4 inches, measured diagonally	Households
Minnesota	2007	Manufacturers of video display devices are responsible for recycling a target amount of covered electronic devices or for paying a recycling fee.	Computers, computer peripherals, facsimile machines, DVD players, video cassette recorders, and video display devices with a screen size greater than 9 inches, measured diagonally	Households
Texas	2008	Manufacturers collect and recycle their own brands. Collection must be convenient and not require a fee at the time of recycling.	Desktop and notebook computers, computer monitors without a tuner, and accompanying mice and keyboards	Individuals who use computer equipment purchased primarily for personal or home business use

Source: GAO analysis of state electronics recycling legislation.

Note: See appendix II of this report for additional information about these five state programs.

In addition, some of these states, as well as some of the states with recycling legislation, have banned certain used electronics, such as CRTs, from landfills. In states with no mechanism to finance the cost of recycling, some local governments that offer recycling bear the recycling costs and others charge fees to consumers. Also, some states have funded voluntary recycling efforts, such as collection events or related efforts organized by local governments. For example, Florida has provided grants to counties in the state to foster the development of an electronics recycling infrastructure.

A variety of entities offer used electronics collection services, either for a fee or at no charge. Localities may organize collection events or collect used electronics at waste transfer stations. A number of electronics manufacturers and retailers support collection events and offer other services. For example, Best Buy offers free recycling of its own branded products and drop-off opportunities for other products at a charge that is offset by a store coupon of the same value; Dell and Goodwill Industries have established a partnership to provide free collection services at many Goodwill donation centers; and a number of electronics manufacturers collect used electronics through mail-back services offered to consumers. Some manufacturers and retailers also have made voluntary commitments to manage used electronics in an environmentally sound manner and to restrict exports of used electronics that they collect for recycling.

EPA Has Contributed to the Sounder Management of Used Electronics, but Its Results Are Limited or Uncertain

EPA has taken some notable steps to augment its enforcement of regulations on exports of CRTs for recycling, but the export of other used electronics remains largely unregulated. In addition, the effect of EPA's partnership programs on the management of used electronics, although positive, is limited or uncertain.

EPA Has Improved Its Enforcement of CRT Export Regulations, but the Export of Other Used Electronics Remains Largely Unregulated

To encourage the recycling and reuse of used CRTs, EPA amended its hazardous waste regulations under the Resource Conservation and Recovery Act by establishing streamlined management requirements. If certain conditions are met, the regulations exclude CRTs from the definition of solid waste and thereby from the regulations that apply to the management of hazardous waste. The conditions include a requirement that exporters of used CRTs for recycling notify EPA of an intended export before the shipments are scheduled to leave the United States and obtain consent from the importing country. In contrast, exporters of used, intact CRTs for reuse (as opposed to recycling) may submit a one-time notification to EPA and are not required to obtain consent from the importing country.[6] The export provisions of the CRT rule became effective in January 2007.

We reported in August 2008 that some companies had appeared to have easily circumvented the CRT rule, and that EPA had done little to enforce it.[7] In particular, we posed as foreign buyers of broken CRTs,[8] and 43 U.S. companies expressed a willingness to export these items. Some of the companies, including ones that publicly touted their exemplary environmental practices, were willing to export CRTs in apparent violation of the CRT rule. Despite the apparently widespread potential for violations, EPA did not issue its first administrative penalty complaint against a company for potentially illegal shipments until the rule had been in effect for 11/2 years, and that penalty came as a result of a problem we had identified. In response to our prior report, EPA officials acknowledged some instances of noncompliance with the CRT rule but stated that, given the rule's relative newness, their focus was on educating the regulated community.

Since our prior report's issuance, however, EPA has initiated investigations and taken several enforcement actions against companies that have violated the notice-and-consent requirement for export of CRTs for recycling. For example, in December 2009, the agency issued an order seeking penalties of up to $37,500 per day to a company that failed to properly manage a shipment of waste CRTs. According to EPA, the company did not provide appropriate notice to the agency or to China, the receiving country, where customs authorities rejected the shipment. Similarly, in December 2009, EPA announced that two companies that failed to notify the agency or receive written consent from China of a shipment of waste CRTs for recycling entered agreements with EPA, with one company agreeing to pay a fine of over $21,000.

Despite steps to strengthen enforcement of the CRT rule, issues related to CRT exports and to exports of other used electronics remain. First, as we reported in August 2008, exports of CRTs for reuse in developing countries have sometimes included broken units that are instead dumped. EPA's CRT rule does not allow such exports and requires that exporters keep copies of normal business records, such as contracts, demonstrating that each shipment of exported CRTs will be reused. However, the rule does not require exporters to test used equipment to verify that it is functional. Moreover, according to EPA, the agency has focused its investigations under the CRT rule on companies that have failed to provide export notifications altogether. In contrast, the agency has not yet conducted any follow-up on notifications of exports for reuse to protect against the dumping of nonworking CRTs in developing countries by ensuring that the CRTs companies are exporting are, in fact, suitable for reuse.

Second, CRTs are the only electronic devices specifically regulated as hazardous waste under EPA's Resource Conservation and Recovery Act regulations.[9] Many other electronic devices, however, contain small amounts of toxic substances, and according to EPA, recent studies have shown that certain used electronics other than CRTs, such as some cell phones, sometime exceed the act's regulatory criteria for toxicity when evaluated using hazardous waste test protocols. Finally, because one of the purposes of the Resource Conservation and Recovery Act is to promote reuse and recovery, EPA's rules under the act exclude used electronics and disassembled component parts that are exported for reuse from the definition of "solid waste" and, therefore, from hazardous waste export requirements, regardless of whether the used electronics exceed the toxicity characteristic regulatory criteria.[10]

EPA's Partnership Programs Have Had a Positive but Limited Effect

EPA has worked with electronics manufacturers, retailers, recyclers, state governments, environmental groups, and other stakeholders to promote partnership programs that address the environmentally sound management of used electronics. In addition, EPA comanages a program to encourage federal agencies and facilities to purchase environmentally preferable electronics and manage used electronics in an environmentally sound manner. Key programs include the following:

- Responsible Recycling practices. EPA convened electronics manufacturers, recyclers, and other stakeholders and provided funding to develop the Responsible Recycling (R2) practices, with the intent that electronics recyclers could obtain certification that they are voluntarily adhering to environmental, worker health and safety, and security practices. Certification to the R2 practices became available in late 2009. According to EPA officials, the R2 practices represent a significant accomplishment in that they provide a means for electronics recyclers to be recognized for voluntary commitments that, according to EPA, go beyond what the agency is able to legally require. The R2 practices identify “focus materials” in used electronics, such as CRTs or items containing mercury, that warrant greater care due to their toxicity or other potential adverse health or environmental effects when managed without the appropriate safeguards. The practices specify that recyclers (and each vendor in the recycling chain) export equipment and components containing focus materials only to countries that legally accept them. The practices also specify that recyclers document the legality of such exports. Upon request by exporters, EPA has agreed to help obtain documentation from foreign governments regarding whether focus materials can be legally imported into their country.

- Plug-In To eCycling. To promote opportunities for individuals to donate or recycle their used consumer electronics, EPA began to partner with electronics manufacturers, retailers, and mobile service providers in 2003. Under the Plug-In To eCycling program, partners commit to ensuring that the electronics refurbishers and recyclers they use follow guidelines developed by EPA for the protection of human health and the environment. Among other things, the current guidelines call for minimizing incineration and landfill disposal and for ensuring that exports comply with requirements in importing countries. According to EPA, Plug-In To eCycling partners have collected and recycled steadily increasing quantities of used electronics,11 and some partners have expanded the collection opportunities they offer to consumers (e.g., from occasional events to permanent locations).
- Electronic Product Environmental Assessment Tool. Developed under a grant from EPA and launched in 2006, the Electronic Product Environmental Assessment Tool (EPEAT) helps purchasers select and compare computers and monitors on the basis of their environmental attributes. EPEAT evaluates electronic products against a set of required and optional criteria in a number of categories, including end-of-life management. To qualify for registration under EPEAT, the sale of all covered products to institutions must include the option to purchase a take-back or recycling service that meets EPA’s Plug-In To eCycling recycling guidelines. Auditing of recycling services against the guidelines is an optional criterion. Currently, EPA is participating with other stakeholders in the development of additional standards covering televisions and imaging equipment, such as copiers and printers.

- Federal Electronics Challenge. To promote the responsible management of electronic products in the federal government, EPA comanages the Federal Electronics Challenge, a program to encourage federal agencies and facilities to purchase environmentally preferable electronic equipment, operate the equipment in an energy-efficient way, and manage used electronics in an environmentally sound manner. According to EPA, partners reported in 2009 that 96 percent of the computer desktops, laptops, and monitors they purchased or leased were EPEAT-registered, and that 83 percent of the electronics they took out of service were reused or recycled. One of the national goals of the Federal Electronics Challenge for 2010 is that 95 percent of the eligible electronic equipment purchased or leased by partnering agencies and facilities be registered under EPEAT. Another goal is that 100 percent of the non-reusable electronic equipment disposed of by partners be recycled using environmentally sound management practices.[12]

While EPA and other stakeholders have contributed to progress in the partnership programs, the impact of the programs on the management of used electronics is limited or uncertain. For example, the Plug-In To eCycling program does not (1) include a mechanism to verify that partners adhere to their commitment to manage used electronics in accordance with EPA's guidelines for the protection of human health and the environment or (2) confirm the quantity of used electronics collected under the program.

In addition, because the development of electronics purchasing and recycling standards is ongoing or only recently completed, it is too soon to determine how the standards will affect the management of used electronics collected from consumers. EPA officials told us that the agency lacks the authority to require electronics recyclers to adhere to the R2 practices, since most electronics are not hazardous waste under Resource Conservation and Recovery Act regulations. EPA participated in the development of the practices through a process open to a range of stakeholders concerned with the management of used electronics. Two environmental groups that participated in the process withdrew their support because the R2 practices failed to address their concerns (e.g., about the export of used electronics). As a result, one of the groups, the Basel Action Network, spearheaded the development of another standard (i.e., e-Stewards®) under which electronics recyclers may be certified on a voluntary basis. EPA is currently considering whether and how to reference such recycler certification standards in other programs, such as Plug-In To eCycling.

Furthermore, EPEAT currently focuses on electronic products sold to institutions but not to individual consumers. In particular, the requirement that manufacturers of EPEAT-registered computers and monitors offer a take-back or recycling service to institutional purchasers does not currently apply to sales to individual consumers. According to an EPA official participating in development of the standards, EPA and other stakeholders plan to begin work in 2010 on expanding the standard for computer equipment into the consumer marketplace, and stakeholders are still discussing whether the new EPEAT standards for imaging equipment and televisions, which will cover electronics sold to individual consumers, will include a required or optional criterion for take back of such electronics.

In October 2009, we reported that an increasing number of federal agencies and facilities has joined the Federal Electronics Challenge, but we also identified opportunities for higher levels of participation and noted that agencies and facilities that participate do not maximize the environmental benefits that can be achieved.[13] We reported, for example, that agencies and facilities representing almost two-thirds of the federal workforce were not program partners, and that only two partners had reported to EPA that they managed electronic products in accordance with the goals for all three life-cycle phases—procurement, operation, and disposal.[14] We concluded that the federal government, which purchases billions of dollars worth of information technology equipment and services annually, has the opportunity to leverage its substantial market power to enhance recycling infrastructures and stimulate markets for environmentally preferable electronic products by broadening and deepening agency and facility participation in the Federal Electronics Challenge. However, EPA has not systematically analyzed the agency's partnership programs, such as the Federal Electronics Challenge, to determine whether the impact of each program could be augmented.

Stakeholders' Views on the State-by-State Approach to Managing Used Electronics Vary Widely

To varying degrees, the entities regulated under the state electronics recycling laws—electronics manufacturers, retailers, and recyclers— consider the increasing number of laws to be a compliance burden. In contrast, in the five states we visited, state and local solid waste management officials expressed varying levels of satisfaction with individual state recycling programs, which they attributed more to the design and implementation of the programs, rather than to any burden caused by the state by state approach. (See app. II for a description of key elements of the electronics recycling programs in the five states.)

Manufacturers, Retailers, and Recyclers View the State-by-State Approach as a Compliance Burden to Varying Degrees

Manufacturers

Electronics manufacturers, retailers, and recyclers described various ways in which they are affected by the current state-by-state approach toward the management of used electronics, with manufacturers expressing the greatest concern about the lack of uniformity.

The scope of manufacturers regulated under state electronics recycling laws, as well as how states define "manufacturer," varies by state. The laws apply to both multinational corporations as well as small companies whose products may not be sold in every state and, depending on the law, to manufacturers of both information technology equipment and televisions. In some states, such as Maine and Washington, the number of regulated manufacturers is over 100.

Because most state electronics recycling laws are based on the producer responsibility model, these laws, by design, assign manufacturers significant responsibility for financing and, in some states, for arranging the collection and recycling of used electronics. As a result, the two electronics manufacturer associations we interviewed, as well as eight of the nine individual manufacturers, told us that the state-by-state approach represents a significant compliance burden. The individual manufacturer that did not consider the state-by-state approach to be a significant burden explained that the company is not currently manufacturing covered electronic devices (specifically televisions) and, therefore, does not have responsibilities under most of the state laws.

Depending on the specific provisions of state laws, examples of the duplicative requirements that individual manufacturers described as burdensome included paying annual registration fees to multiple state governments, submitting multiple reports to state environmental agencies, reviewing and paying invoices submitted by multiple recyclers, and conducting legal analyses of state laws to determine the responsibilities placed on manufacturers. A representative of a manufacturer of information technology equipment said that, due to the time needed to ensure compliance with differing state laws, the company cannot spend time on related activities, such as finding ways to reduce the cost of complying with the state laws or ensuring that electronics are recycled in an environmentally sound manner.

Representatives of one manufacturer noted that even states with similar versions of producer responsibility legislation differ in terms of specific requirements, such as the scope of covered electronic devices, registration and reporting deadlines, and the types of information to be submitted. As a result, they said that they needed to conduct separate compliance efforts for each state, rather than implement a single compliance program. A few manufacturers also told us that their current compliance costs are in the millions of dollars and are increasing as more states enact electronics recycling legislation. For example, a Sony representative said that he expects the amount the company spends in 2010 to comply with the requirements in states with producer responsibility laws to increase almost sevenfold over the amount spent in 2008.

While the producer responsibility model is based on the assumption that manufacturers pass along the cost of recycling to consumers in the form of higher prices, the electronics manufacturer associations, as well as individual manufacturers, described inefficiencies and higher costs created by the state-by-state approach that they said could be reduced through a uniform national approach. For example, the Consumer Electronics Association cited a 2006 report, which the association helped fund, on the costs that could be avoided under a hypothetical, single national approach.[15] The report estimated that, with 20 different state programs, manufacturers would spend an additional $41 million each year, and that the total additional annual costs among all stakeholders— including manufacturers, retailers, recyclers, and state governments— would be about $125 million.

Both the Consumer Electronics Association, most of whose members the association considers to be small electronics manufacturers, as well as the Information Technology Industry Council, which represents large manufacturers, told us that some provisions of state laws—such as registration fees that do not take into account the number of covered electronic devices sold in a state—can create a disproportionate burden on small manufacturers. For example, Maine's law imposes a $3,000 annual registration fee on all manufacturers, regardless of size or sales volume. One small manufacturer told us that Maryland's initial registration fee of $10,000 exceeded the company's $200 profits from sales in the state. The manufacturer said that, if all 50 states imposed such fees, the company would not remain in business. Similarly, the need to analyze differing requirements in each state law requires staff resources that, unlike their larger counterparts, small manufacturers may lack.

Despite the costs of complying with state electronics recycling legislation, representatives of the two electronics manufacturer associations we interviewed, as well as most of the individual manufacturers, told us that state laws based on the producer responsibility model have not led to the design of electronic products that are less toxic and more recyclable, which some states cite as one of the purposes for making manufacturers responsible for the management of used electronics. Manufacturers cited the following reasons for the lack of an impact on product design:

- the inability of manufacturers to anticipate how recycling practices and technologies may develop over time and incorporate those developments into the design of products that may be discarded only after years of use;
- some producer responsibility laws, such as in Minnesota and Washington, making individual manufacturers responsible for recycling not their own products but a general category of devices, including those designed by other manufacturers; and
- the greater impact of other factors on product design, such as consumer demand and the use by institutional purchasers of EPEAT to select and compare electronic devices on the basis of their environmental attributes.

Retailers

Retailers generally affected by state electronics recycling laws include national chains as well as small electronics shops. Some retailers, such as Best Buy, sell their own brand of covered electronic devices and are also classified as manufacturers under certain states' laws. As an example of the number of retailers covered under the laws, information from the state of California indicates that over 15,000 retailers have registered to collect the state's recycling fee, and state officials estimated that large retailers collect 80 percent of the revenues.

While the requirements imposed by state electronics recycling legislation on retailers typically are less extensive than the requirements pertaining to manufacturers, representatives of national and state retail associations we

interviewed, as well as individual electronics retailers, described ways that the state-by-state approach creates a compliance burden. For example, according to the Consumer Electronics Retailers Coalition, certain state requirements, such as prohibitions on selling the products of electronics manufacturers that have not complied with a state's law, are difficult for large retailers to implement since they do not use state-specific networks for distributing products to their stores. Rather, electronic products are developed, marketed, and sold on a national and even global basis.

Similarly, representatives of the Consumer Electronics Retailers Coalition, as well as the majority of individual retailers and state retail associations in the five states we visited, told us that state "point-of-sale" requirements to collect a fee (in California) or distribute information on recycling when consumers purchase an electronic product represents a burden (e.g., many retailers operate their point-of-sale systems out of a centralized location yet are required to meet differing requirements in each state). Some retailers also expressed concern that states have difficulty in enforcing requirements on Internet retailers and, as a result, that businesses with a physical presence in the state are disadvantaged. This point is supported by the Maine Department of Environmental Protection, which has indicated that the department lacks sufficient staff to ensure that retailers that sell exclusively on the Internet comply with the sales ban on products from noncompliant manufacturers.

Retailers also expressed concerns over specific provisions of individual state laws. For example, representatives of the California Retailers Association said their members consider the state's requirement to collect a recycling fee at the point of sale and remit the fee to the state to be particularly burdensome, even though the law allows retailers to retain 3 percent of the fee as reimbursement for their costs. One retailer explained that collecting the fee also generates resentment against the retailer among customers who are unaware of the state's recycling law. Similarly, according to the Minnesota Retailers Association, retailers found it challenging to gather and report accurate sales data required to calculate manufacturer recycling targets under the state's law. In response to concerns over collecting and reporting sales data, Minnesota amended its law to eliminate this requirement and to use national sales data instead.

Retailers that sell their own brand of covered electronic devices and are classified as manufacturers under a particular state's law must meet all requirements imposed on either type of entity. Similarly, Best Buy and other retailers that offer customers a take-back service for used electronics are considered authorized collectors under some state programs and, as a result, are subject to additional registration and reporting requirements. Best Buy officials told us they face unique challenges under the state-by-state approach because they participate in programs as a retailer; a manufacturer; and, in some cases, a collector. For example, the officials cited 47 annual reporting and registration deadlines to comply with requirements imposed on manufacturers, 19 annual reporting or review dates associated with retailer requirements, and 6 annual reporting or registration dates associated with collector requirements.

Recyclers

Electronics recyclers range from large multinational corporations to small entities with a location in one state and encompass a range of business models. For example, some recyclers focus on "asset disposition"—that is, providing data destruction and computer refurbishment services to businesses and large institutions—and other recyclers focus on recovering valuable commodities, such as precious metals. The use of "downstream" vendors to process various components separated from electronics is common, and many of the downstream entities, such as those that recycle glass from CRTs, are located overseas. Numerous nonprofit organizations refurbish used computers for use by schools, low-income families, and other nonprofit organizations both in the United States and overseas.

The degree to which the recyclers we interviewed expressed concerns about the state-by-state approach varied. While state laws have established differing registration, reporting, and record-keeping requirements for recyclers and, where specified, different methods of payment for the cost of recycling or collection, some recyclers said they are not generally impacted by such differences (e.g., they operate in only one state with electronics recycling legislation or they can cope with differing state requirements for environmentally sound management by adhering to the most stringent requirements). One recycler even pointed out that the existence of various state laws can create business opportunities. In particular, rather than attempt to develop their own programs to comply with differing state requirements, manufacturers may decide to contract with recyclers that may have greater familiarity with the provisions of different laws.

In contrast, other recyclers expressed concern over the burden of meeting the requirements of differing state laws. Due to the differences among state laws and the programs as implemented, these recyclers may have to carry out different tasks in each state to be reimbursed, such as counting and sorting covered electronic devices by brand and invoicing individual manufacturers;

marketing and selling the amount of used electronics they have processed to manufacturers that must meet recycling targets; and, in California, submitting recycling payment claims to the state government. One recycler told us that the differences among state laws create a disincentive for establishing operations in other states, while another mentioned how small variations among state laws can significantly affect a recycler's capacity to do business in a state. Another recycler added that the state-by-state approach hinders the processing of large volumes of used electronics from households and the ability to generate economies of scale that would reduce recycling costs.

Almost all of the electronics recyclers we interviewed, including those in each of the five states we studied in detail, told us that they are concerned about the ability of irresponsible recyclers to easily enter and undercut the market by charging low prices without processing the material in an environmentally sound manner. While such undercutting might persist even under a national approach to managing used electronics, the recyclers identified a number of factors in the state-by-state approach that magnify the problem, including their perception of a lack of enforcement by state environmental agencies. In addition, according to recyclers in California and Washington, some recyclers export—rather than domestically recycle—electronic devices not covered under the state laws, which is less costly and thereby gives them a competitive advantage over recyclers that do not engage in exports, even where legal.

Some recyclers and refurbishers of used electronics told us that state laws foster recycling at the expense of reuse, even though refurbishment and reuse is viewed by EPA as being more environmentally friendly than recycling. Specifically, according to these stakeholders, some state programs focus on collecting and recycling used electronics but not refurbishing them, thereby creating a financial incentive to recycle used electronics that could otherwise be refurbished and reused. For example, in Minnesota, only the amount in weight of collected used electronics that is recycled counts toward manufacturers' performance targets. According to one refurbisher in the state, this provision leads to the recycling of equipment that is in working condition and reusable. Similarly, California pays for the cost of collecting and recycling used electronics but not for refurbishment. In contrast, according to a Texas affiliate of Goodwill Industries that recycles and refurbishes used electronics, the state's law promotes reuse of used electronics. For example, by requiring that manufacturers establish take-back programs but not setting recycling targets, the Texas law avoids creating an incentive to recycle used electronics that can be refurbished.

State and Local Governments Are Mainly Concerned with the Success of Their Individual Recycling Programs

In the five states that we selected for detailed review, state and local government officials expressed varying levels of satisfaction with their electronics recycling laws. In addition, while some state and local governments had participated in the National Electronics Product Stewardship Initiative in an attempt to develop a national financing system for electronics reuse and recycling, the state and local officials we interviewed generally said that the state-by-state approach had not hindered the successful implementation of electronics recycling programs in their jurisdictions. Rather, they attributed their level of satisfaction to the design of the programs, such as the degree to which the programs provide a financing source for collecting and recycling used electronics and the effectiveness of efforts to educate consumers.

None of the five states had statewide data on collection rates prior to implementation of the electronics recycling programs to quantify the impact of the laws, but state and local officials provided a variety of anecdotal information to illustrate the laws' impact, such as collection rates in local communities and trends in the dumping of used electronics on roadsides and other areas.[16] Moreover, the experiences described by state and local officials in the five states illustrate that both general financing models—producer responsibility and a recycling fee paid by consumers—are viable and have the potential to ensure convenient collection opportunities.

Local solid waste management officials in the five states we visited expressed varying levels of satisfaction with state electronics recycling legislation in terms of reducing their burden of managing used electronics. On one hand, local officials in Washington told us that the state's law requiring that manufacturers establish a convenient collection network for the recycling of used electronics has been successful in increasing collection opportunities and relieving local governments of recycling costs. Similarly, local officials in California said the state's use of a recycling fee for reimbursing collection and recycling costs had relieved their governments of the burden of managing used electronics by making it profitable for the private sector to provide collection and recycling services. On the other hand, according to local solid waste management officials in Texas, the lack of specific criteria in the provision of the state's law requiring that manufacturers collect their own brands of used computer equipment limited the law's impact on increasing the convenience of collection opportunities. In addition, the officials said the state government had not done enough to educate residents about the law. As a result, they said that local governments were still bearing the burden of managing used computer equipment.

State and local solid waste management officials we interviewed from three states without electronics recycling legislation also expressed varying levels of satisfaction with their voluntary efforts to promote recycling under the state-by-state approach to managing used electronics. For example, a county hazardous waste coordinator in Florida said the county used funding from the state to establish an electronics recycling program that is self-sustaining and free to households, but he also said that the state-by-state approach is cumbersome. Similarly, Florida state officials said that every state county has recycling opportunities, although collection could be more convenient. A representative of the Association of State and Territorial Solid Waste Management Officials said that, without a mechanism to finance the cost of recycling used electronics, local governments that provide recycling opportunities may be bearing the cost of providing such services, which can impose a financial burden on communities. In addition, while most of the state and local officials we interviewed from states without legislation said that the state-by-state approach does not represent a burden, Arizona state officials pointed out an increased burden of ensuring the environmentally sound management of used electronics collected in a neighboring state (California) and shipped to their state, since California has an electronic waste law, but Arizona does not.

While state environmental officials we interviewed agreed that the burden of the state-by-state approach falls primarily on the regulated industries, they also acknowledged a number of aspects of the state-by-state approach that limit or complicate their own efforts, including the following:

- *The need to ensure that state programs do not pay for the recycling of used electronics from out of state.* In California, where the state reimburses recyclers $0.39 per pound for the cost of collecting and recycling covered electronic devices, state environmental officials said that they have regularly denied 2 to 5 percent of the claims submitted by recyclers due to problems with documentation, and that some portion of the denied claims likely represents fraudulent claims for the recycling of used electronics collected from other states. To prevent the recycling fee paid by consumers in the state from being used to finance the cost of recycling used electronics from other states, California requires that collectors of used electronics (other than local governments or their agents) maintain a log that includes the name and address of persons who discard covered electronic devices, and the state checks the logs to ensure that it pays only for the recycling of devices generated within the state. California state officials responsible for implementing the electronics recycling legislation said that the time spent on ensuring this requirement is met is a significant contributor to their workload. State and local government officials in other states we visited also acknowledged the potential for their programs to finance the recycling of used electronics collected from out of state, but these officials did not consider the problem to be widespread or difficult to address. For example, a Maine official said that, as a standard practice, waste collection facilities in the state check the residency of individuals, including when the facilities collect used electronics for recycling.

- Ability to ensure compliance with state requirements for environmentally sound management. State environmental officials in the five states we visited described varying levels of oversight to ensure the environmentally sound management of used electronics collected under their programs. For example, California conducts annual inspections of recyclers approved under the state program. Among other things, the state's inspection checklist covers the packaging and labeling of electronic devices, the training of personnel on how to handle waste, the tracking of waste shipments, and the procedures and protective equipment needed to manage the hazards associated with the treatment of electronic devices. In contrast, citing limited resources, officials in Minnesota said they rely on spot checks of large recyclers, and officials in Texas said they have prioritized regular, scheduled enforcement of other environmental regulations over the requirements adopted by the state for the recycling of electronics. Even in California, state officials said that their ability to ensure the environmentally sound management of waste shipped out of state is limited because, while covered devices must be dismantled in California to be eligible for a claim within the state's payment system, residuals from the in-state dismantling and treatment of covered devices may be shipped out of state. Intact but noncovered electronic devices are not subject to the California program and hence may also be shipped out of state. The problem is exacerbated because many of the "downstream" vendors used to process materials separated from electronics are located overseas, which further limits the ability of state officials to ensure that recyclers are conducting due diligence on downstream vendors and that the materials are being managed in an environmentally sound manner. (See app. II for additional information on the requirements for environmentally sound management in the five states we studied in detail.)

Environmental Groups Cited the Accomplishments of State Electronics Recycling Programs but Acknowledged Limitations in States' Ability to Address Exports

In each of the five states we visited, state environmental nonprofit organizations either advocated for the enactment of state electronics recycling legislation or have been active in tracking the implementation of the laws. In addition, a number of groups advocate on issues related to the management of used electronics on a national or international basis. For example, the Electronics TakeBack Coalition, which includes a number of nonprofit organizations, advocates for producer responsibility as a policy for promoting responsible recycling in the electronics industry, and the Basel Action Network works in opposition to exports of toxic wastes to developing counties.

Like state and local government officials in the five states we visited, state environmental groups we interviewed described the design of the state recycling programs, rather than the state-by-state approach, as the primary factor in the success of the programs.

Representatives of the state environmental groups in four of the five states—California, Maine, Minnesota, and Washington—said that they considered their state program to have been successful in providing convenient collection opportunities and in increasing the collection rates of used electronics.

For example, citing a 2007 survey of Maine municipalities, a representative of the Natural Resources Council of Maine said that the collection opportunities under the state program are more convenient than anticipated, although convenience could be improved for some state residents. Similarly, a representative of Californians Against Waste said that the state's recycling fee had resulted in convenient collection opportunities and in steadily increasing collection rates, and that a recycling fee paid by consumers is no less effective than the producer responsibility model in promoting the collection of used electronics.

In contrast, echoing the results of a 2009 survey conducted by the organization, a Texas Campaign for the Environment representative said that the state's law had not had a significant impact on the collection and recycling of used electronics, because both consumers and local solid waste management officials are unaware of the opportunities manufacturers are to provide under the law for the free collection and recycling of electronics discarded by households. In addition, the organization is critical of the fact that the Texas law does not cover televisions, and that the governor vetoed a bill that would have made television manufacturers responsible for recycling, including costs.

Some environmental groups pointed out that, in and of itself, the ability of a state program to improve collection rates does not necessarily ensure that used electronics will be recycled in an environmentally sound manner. Key issues raised by environmental groups as complicating the effectiveness of state programs included a lack of adequate requirements for the environmentally sound management of used electronics or requirements that differ among states, limited state resources or oversight to ensure compliance with the requirements, and a lack of authority to address concerns about exports.

For example, a representative of the Basel Action Network said that provisions in state laws regarding exports, such as those in California, could be challenged on constitutional grounds since the Constitution generally gives the federal government the authority to regulate commerce with foreign nations, thereby limiting states' authorities to do so.

Options for Promoting the Environmentally Sound Management of Used Electronics Involve Basic Policy Considerations

Options to further promote the environmentally sound management of used electronics involve a number of basic policy considerations and encompass many variations. For the purposes of this report, we examined two endpoints on the spectrum of variations: (1) a continued reliance on state recycling programs supplemented by EPA's partnership programs and (2) the establishment of federal standards for state electronics recycling programs. Further federal regulation of electronic waste exports is a potential component of either of these two approaches.

Continued Reliance on State Recycling Programs Supplemented by EPA's Partnership Programs

Under a national approach for managing used electronics on the basis of a continuation of the current state-by-state approach, EPA's partnership programs, such as Plug-In To eCycling, would supplement state efforts. Most used electronics would continue to be managed as solid waste under the Resource Conservation and Recovery Act, with a limited federal role. For example, beyond its establishment of minimum standards for solid waste landfills, EPA is authorized to provide technical assistance to state and local governments for the development of solid waste management plans and to develop suggested guidelines for solid waste management.

EPA's partnership programs can supplement state recycling efforts in a variety of ways. For example, Minnesota state environmental officials told us that they hope to incorporate the R2 practices into the state's standards for the environmentally sound management of used electronics. However, as we have previously noted, the impact of the EPA's promotion of partnership programs on the management of used electronics is limited or uncertain. Moreover, EPA does not have a plan for coordinating its efforts with state electronics recycling programs or for articulating how EPA's partnership programs, taken together, can best assist stakeholders to achieve the environmentally sound management of used electronics. For example, while partnership programs such as Plug-In To eCycling can complement state programs, EPA does not have a plan for leveraging such programs to promote recycling opportunities in states without electronics recycling legislation.

Key Implications of a Continuation of the State-byState Approach

Among the key implications of a continuation of the state-by-state approach are a greater flexibility for states and a continuation of a patchwork of state recycling efforts, including some states with no electronics recycling requirements.

Greater Flexibility for States

This approach provides states with the greatest degree of flexibility to engage in recycling efforts that suit their particular needs and circumstances, whether through legislation or other mechanisms, such as grants for local communities. For example,according to local solid waste management officials in Texas, which has enacted electronics recycling legislation, the state has not banned the disposal of electronics in landfills, and the officials pointed to factors, such as the state's landfill capacity, that would work against a landfill ban. In contrast, New Hampshire, which has limited landfill capacity, has banned the disposal of certain electronics in landfills but has not enacted a law that finances the recycling of used electronics.[17] The state's solid waste management official told us that the state's approach had been successful in diverting a large amount of used electronics from disposal in landfills, and an official with the state's municipal association told us that residents of the state accept that they must pay fees to cover the cost of waste disposal services, including electronics recycling. A state-by-state approach also allows for innovations among states in enacting electronics recycling legislation. For example, a representative of the Electronics TakeBack Coalition told us that state electronics recycling legislation can be effective in providing convenient collection opportunities and in increasing collection and recycling rates, but that more time is needed to be able to assess the impact of the state programs. The representative described the state programs as laboratories for testing variations in the models on which the programs are based, such as the use of recycling targets in the producer responsibility model, and for allowing the most effective variations to be identified.

A Continuation of the Patchwork of State Recycling Efforts

While the state-by-state approach may provide states with greater regulatory flexibility, it does not address the concerns of manufacturers and other stakeholders who consider the state-by-state approach to be a significant compliance burden. The compliance burden may actually worsen as more states enact laws (e.g., the number of registration and reporting requirements imposed on manufacturers may increase). One manufacturer pointed out that, while some states have modeled their laws on those in other states, even in such cases, states may make changes to the model in ways that limit any efficiency from the similarities among multiple laws. In addition to creating a compliance burden, the state-by-state approach does not ensure a baseline in terms of promoting the environmentally sound reuse and recycling of used electronics, not only in states without electronics recycling legislation but also in states with legislation. For example, unlike some other state electronics recycling legislation, the Texas law does not require manufacturers to finance the recycling of televisions, which may require a cost incentive for recycling, since the cost of managing the leaded glass from televisions with CRTs may exceed the value of materials recycled from used equipment. Furthermore, the requirements for the environmentally sound management of used electronics vary among states, and state environmental agencies engage in varying levels of oversight to ensure environmentally sound management. For example, according to the state solid waste management official in New Hampshire, budget constraints prevent the state from being able to track what happens to used electronics after they are collected.

Stakeholder Efforts to Ease the Compliance Burden of the State-by-State Approach

Various stakeholder efforts are under way to help coordinate state programs and relieve the compliance burden, although some stakeholders have pointed to limitations of such efforts. In particular, in January 2010, a number of state environmental agencies and electronics manufacturers, retailers, and recyclers helped form the Electronics Recycling Coordination Clearinghouse, a forum for coordination and information exchange among the state and local agencies that are implementing electronics recycling laws and all impacted stakeholders.[18] Examples of activities planned under the clearinghouse include collecting and maintaining data on collection volumes and creating a centralized location for receiving and processing manufacturer registrations and reports required under state laws. Other examples of stakeholder efforts to ease the compliance burden include the formation of the Electronic Manufacturers Recycling Management Company, a consortium of manufacturers that collaborate to develop recycling programs in states with electronics recycling legislation. In addition, individual states have made changes to their recycling programs' legislation after identifying provisions in their laws that created unnecessary burdens for particular stakeholders. For example, Minnesota amended its law to remove the requirement that retailers annually report to each manufacturer the number of the manufacturer's covered electronic devices sold to households in the state—a requirement that retailers found particularly burdensome.

A number of stakeholders, however, including members of the Electronics Recycling Coordination Clearinghouse, have pointed to limitations of stakeholder efforts to coordinate state electronics recycling programs. According to representatives of the Consumer Electronics Association, concerns over federal antitrust provisions limit cooperation among manufacturers for the purpose of facilitating compliance with the state laws. For example, cooperation among manufacturers trying to minimize the cost of compliance would raise concerns among electronics recyclers about price-fixing. Similarly, the executive director of the National Center for Electronics Recycling, which manages the Electronics Recycling Coordination Clearinghouse, told us states are unlikely to make changes to harmonize basic elements of state laws that currently differ, such as the scope of covered electronic devices and the definitions of terms such as "manufacturer."[19]

Establishment of Federal Standards for Electronics Recycling Programs

Under a national strategy based on the establishment of federal standards for state electronics recycling programs, federal legislation would be required. For the purpose of analysis, we assumed that the legislation would establish federal standards and provide for their implementation— for example, through a cooperative federalism approach whereby states could opt to assume responsibility for the standards or leave implementation to EPA, through incentives for states to develop complying programs, or through a combination of these options. Within this alternative, there are many issues that would need to be addressed. A primary issue of concern to many stakeholders is the degree to which the federal government would (1) establish minimum standards, allowing states to adopt stricter standards (thereby providing states with flexibility but also potentially increasing the compliance burden from the standpoint of regulated entities), or (2) establish fixed standards. Further issues include whether federal standards would focus on the elements of state electronics recycling laws that are potentially less controversial and have a likelihood of achieving efficiencies—such as data collection and manufacturer reporting and registration—or would focus on all of the elements, building on lessons learned from the various states.

Issue of Establishing Minimum Federal Standards versus Fixed Federal Standards

An overriding issue of concern to many stakeholders is the degree to which federal standards would be established as minimum standards, fixed standards, or some combination of the two. In this context, we have assumed that either minimum or fixed standards would, by definition, preempt less stringent state laws and lead to the establishment of programs in states that have not enacted electronics recycling legislation. Minimum standards would be intended to ensure that programs in every state met baseline requirements established by the federal government, while allowing flexibility to states that have enacted legislation meeting the minimum standards to continue with existing programs, some of which are well-established. In contrast, under fixed federal standards, states would not be able to establish standards either stricter or more lenient than the federal standards. Thus, fixed standards would offer relatively little flexibility, although states would still have regulatory authority in areas not covered by the federal standards.

As we have previously reported,[20] minimum standards are often designed to provide a baseline in areas such as environmental protection, vehicle safety, and working conditions. For example, a national approach based on minimum standards would be consistent with the authority given to EPA to regulate hazardous waste management under the Resource Conservation and Recovery Act, which allows for state requirements that are more stringent than those imposed by EPA. Such a strategy can be an option when the national objective requires that common minimum standards be in place in every state, but stricter state standards are workable. Conversely, fixed standards are an option when stricter state standards are not workable. For example, to provide national uniformity and thereby facilitate the increased collection and recycling of certain batteries, the Mercury-Containing and Rechargeable Battery Management Act does not allow states the option of establishing more stringent regulations regarding collection, storage, and transportation, although states can adopt and enforce standards for the recycling and disposal of such batteries that are more stringent than existing federal standards under the Resource Conservation and Recovery Act.

Most manufacturers we interviewed told us they prefer fixed federal standards over minimum standards. For example, these manufacturers are concerned that many states would opt to exceed the minimum federal standards, leaving manufacturers responsible for complying with differing requirements, not only in the states that have electronics recycling legislation but also in the states currently without legislation. In contrast, most state government officials and environmental groups we interviewed told us that they would prefer minimum federal standards over fixed federal standards as a national approach for the management of used electronics. In addition, a representative of the National Conference of State Legislatures told us that the organization generally opposes federal preemption but accepts that in the area of environmental policy, the federal government often sets minimum standards. According to the representative, even if federal requirements were of a high standard, states may want the option to impose tougher standards if the need arises. Similarly, some legislative and executive branch officials in states with electronics recycling legislation expressed concern that federal standards for electronics recycling would be of a low standard. As a result, the officials said they want to preserve the ability of states to impose more stringent requirements.

To help address manufacturer concerns about a continuation of the state-by-state approach under minimum standards, the federal government could encourage states not to exceed those standards. For example, establishing minimum standards that are relatively stringent might reduce the incentive for states to enact or maintain stricter requirements.

Consistent with this view, some of the state electronics recycling laws, including those in four of the five states we studied in detail, contain provisions for discontinuing the state program if a federal law takes effect that meets specified conditions (e.g., establishing an equivalent national program).

Other Issues to Consider in Establishing Federal Standards

Based on our review of state electronics recycling legislation and discussions with stakeholders regarding a national strategy for the management of used electronics, we identified a range of issues that would need to be considered and could be addressed as part of the establishment of federal standards for state electronics recycling programs, including the following issues:

The Financing of Recycling Costs

A potential element in federal standards for state electronics recycling programs would be a mechanism for financing the cost of recycling. For example, representatives of the Consumer Electronics Association told us they support a national approach with a single financing mechanism. Similarly, the California and Washington laws stipulate that their programs be discontinued if a federal law takes effect that establishes a national program, but only if the federal law provides a financing mechanism for the collection and recycling of all electronic devices covered under their respective laws. While there are differences among their views, most stakeholders we interviewed, including some manufacturers, said they would prefer that any federal standards be based on some form of the producer responsibility model rather than on a recycling fee paid by consumers because, for example, they consider the producer responsibility model more efficient to implement in comparison with the resources devoted to collecting a recycling fee and reimbursing recyclers. Even California state government officials, who were generally pleased with what has been accomplished under the state's recycling fee and payment model, expressed openness to the producer responsibility model. The level of support for producer responsibility represents a shift in the views of some manufacturers. In particular, representatives of the Information Technology Industry Council told us that television manufacturers previously supported a recycling fee paid by consumers because of the frequent turnover of television manufacturers and the problem of assigning recycling costs for legacy equipment whose original manufacturer is no longer in business, no longer makes televisions, or otherwise cannot be determined. According to the council, with only one state having enacted legislation based on a recycling fee, television and other manufacturers now support the producer responsibility model.

The Allocation of Costs and Responsibilities among Stakeholders

Even under a producer responsibility model, stakeholders other than manufacturers would participate in the implementation of state electronics recycling legislation, and the costs of collecting and recycling used electronics can be assigned in different ways. For example, while they support the producer responsibility model, Information Technology Industry Council representatives have proposed that the model be based on "shared responsibility," whereby various entities that profit from the sale of electronic devices—including electronics distributors, retailers, and other stakeholders—all contribute to the cost of collection and recycling. In a variation of the concept of shared responsibility, under Maine's electronics recycling legislation participating local governments generally bear collection costs and manufacturers finance recycling costs. The way in which costs and responsibilities are allocated can also create inequities from the standpoint of certain stakeholders. For example, certain manufacturers may pay more or less than others depending on whether recycling costs are based on the weight of a manufacturer's own brand of electronics collected for recycling (return share) or on the amount of a manufacturer's new products sold (market share). Under a return share system, long-standing manufacturers bear a greater proportion of the costs in comparison with newer manufacturers with fewer used electronics in the waste stream. In contrast, a market share system can result in newer manufacturers with a large market share financing the recycling of products produced by their competitors.

The Division of Federal and State Responsibilities for Implementation and Enforcement

Federal standards can be implemented directly by a federal agency, by the states with some degree of federal oversight, or through state implementation in some states and direct federal implementation in others. For example, EPA develops hazardous waste regulations under the Resource Conservation and Recovery Act and has encouraged states to assume primary responsibility for implementation and enforcement through state adoption of the regulations, while EPA retains independent enforcement authority. Regarding used electronics, the division of responsibilities among the federal and state governments would have a direct bearing on EPA's resource requirements. EPA has previously cautioned that assigning responsibilities to the agency—such as for registration of electronics manufacturers, retailers, and recyclers; collection of registration fees; approval of manufacturer recycling programs; and authorization of parallel state programs for electronics recycling—would be costly and time-consuming to implement. Similarly, a representative of the National Conference of State Legislatures said the organization would oppose any federal requirements that do not provide a source of funding to states for implementing the requirements, and a representative of the National Governors Association pointed out that states not currently having electronics recycling legislation would express concern about the administrative costs of implementing an electronics recycling program.

Determination of the Scope of Covered Electronic Devices

Stakeholders have cited a variety of criteria for determining the scope of electronic devices covered by state recycling laws. For example, some stakeholders have cited the growing volume of used electronics in comparison with limited landfill capacity or the presence of toxic substances in many electronics.

In contrast, other stakeholders have argued that cell phones and other mobile devices, which may contain toxic substances, should not be included with other used electronics (e.g., mobile devices can be easily collected through mail-back programs). As yet another alternative, stakeholders have cited the loss of valuable resources, such as precious metals, when used electronics are disposed in landfills, as well as the environmental benefits of extending the life of used electronics through refurbishment, as a key consideration in electronics recycling legislation.

An issue closely related to the scope of covered electronic devices is the scope of entities whose used electronics are covered under programs for financing the cost of recycling.

The state electronics recycling laws typically include used electronics from households, but some states also include other entities, such as small businesses and nonprofit organizations that may otherwise need to pay a fee to recycle used electronics in an environmentally sound manner, while California's law is nontargeted and includes any user of a covered electronic device located within the state.

Further Federal Regulation of Exports Is a Potential Component of Either Approach to Managing Used Electronics

In doing our work, we found that a potential component of either approach that we discuss for managing used electronics is a greater federal regulatory role over exports to (1) facilitate coordination with other countries to reduce the possibility of unsafe recycling or dumping and (2) address the limitations on the authority of states to regulate exports. Assuming a continuation of the factors that contribute to exports, such as a limited domestic infrastructure to recycle used electronics, an increase in collection rates resulting from electronics recycling laws, either at the state or federal level, is likely to lead to a corresponding increase in exports, absent any federal restrictions. While, as we have previously noted, exports can be handled responsibly in countries with effective regulatory regimes and by companies with advanced technologies, some of the increase in exports may end up in countries that lack safe recycling and disposal capacity.

Exports of used electronics are subject to a range of state requirements and guidelines in the five states we visited. Nevertheless, many of the state officials we interviewed expressed support for federal action to limit harmful exports because, for example, states lack adequate authority and resources to address concerns about exports. Washington state officials noted that their governor vetoed a provision of the state's electronic waste legislation that addressed exports of electronics collected under the program because of concerns about the state's lack of authority to prohibit such exports. The governor instead called for federal legislation prohibiting the export of hazardous waste to countries that are not prepared to manage the waste. In addition, under "preferred standards" established by the state, recyclers can be contractually obligated to ensure that countries legally accept any imports of materials of concern. Washington state officials told us that establishing preferred standards helped the state partially address concerns about used electronics exports, notwithstanding potential limitations on the state's authority, but that further federal regulation of exports would still be helpful.

In our August 2008 report,[21] we made two recommendations to EPA to strengthen the federal role in reducing harmful exports. First, we recommended that EPA consider ways to broaden its regulations under existing Resource Conservation and Recovery Act authority to address the export of used electronic devices that might not be classified as hazardous waste by current U.S. regulations but might threaten human health and the environment when unsafely disassembled overseas. For example, we suggested that EPA consider expanding the scope of the CRT rule to cover other exported used electronics and revising the regulatory definition of hazardous waste. Citing the time and legal complexities involved in broadening its regulations under the Resource Conservation and Recovery Act, EPA disagreed with our recommendation and instead expressed the agency's support for addressing concerns about exports of used electronics through nonregulatory, voluntary approaches. However, EPA officials told us that the agency is taking another look at its existing authorities to regulate exports of other used electronics.

Second, we recommended that the agency submit to Congress a legislative package for ratification of the Basel Convention on the Control of Transboundary Movements of Hazardous Wastes and Their Disposal, a multilateral environmental agreement that aims to protect against the adverse effects resulting from transboundary movements of hazardous waste. Under the convention's definition, a broader range of materials could be considered potentially hazardous, including some electronic devices. While the Senate provided its advice and consent to ratification in 1992, successive administrations have not submitted draft legislation to Congress giving EPA the necessary statutory authorities to implement the convention's requirements in order to complete the ratification process. EPA officials explained that these needed additional authorities include, among others, the authority to control the scope of wastes covered by the Basel Convention, the authority to halt exports of hazardous waste if the agency believes they will not be handled in an environmentally sound manner, and the authority to take back shipments that cannot be handled in an environmentally sound manner in the importing country. EPA officials told us that the agency had developed a legislative proposal on more than one occasion under previous administrations but did not finalize any proposal with other federal agencies. According to these officials, finalizing the proposal requires coordination with a number of agencies, including the Department of State and the White House Council on Environmental Quality, which coordinates federal environmental efforts in the development of environmental policies and initiatives.

In May 2010, the current EPA Administrator called for legislative changes to address exports and for taking steps toward ratification of the Basel Convention. EPA officials have also cited a number of benefits of ratifying the Basel Convention, such as the ability to fully participate in convention decisions on issues related to the environmentally sound management of used electronics. For example, according to EPA officials, upcoming convention decisions on guidelines for environmentally sound refurbishment and repair will impact parties' export of used electronics for reuse, which is regarded by refurbishers as environmentally preferable to recycling but also raises concerns about the dumping of used electronics in developing countries. Basel Convention working groups on environmentally sound management are open to a range of participants that do not represent parties to the convention, including EPA, electronics manufacturers, electronics recyclers and refurbishers, and environmental groups. However, given that the United States is a signatory but not a party to the convention, the United States does not participate in the final decisions on issues such as environmentally sound management. EPA officials said they anticipate a number of such decisions in the next few years, especially regarding the transboundary movement of used and endof-life electronics.

According to EPA officials, a greater federal regulatory role over exports resulting from ratification of the Basel Convention would require an increase in EPA's programmatic and enforcement resources, such as additional staff. The additional resources would be needed to enable the Administrator to determine whether proposed exports will be conducted in an environmentally sound manner and to implement the Basel Convention's notice-and-consent requirement. Moreover, the European Union's experience under the waste electrical and electronic equipment directive, which contains an obligation for waste equipment to be treated in ways that avoid environmental harm, demonstrates the need to couple the regulation of exports with enforcement efforts. A European Commission report estimated that 50 percent of waste equipment that is collected is probably not being treated in line with the directive's objectives and requirements, and that a large volume of waste may be illegally shipped to developing countries, where it is dumped or recycled in ways that are dangerous to human health and the environment.

CONCLUSION

Broad agreement exists among key stakeholders that reusing and recycling electronics in an environmentally sound manner has substantial advantages over disposing of them in landfills or exporting them to developing countries in a manner that threatens human health and the environment. There has been much debate over the best way to promote environmentally sound reuse and recycling, however, and any national approach may entail particular advantages and disadvantages for stakeholders. While empirical information about the experiences of states and other stakeholders in their efforts to manage used electronics can inform this debate, the question of a national approach revolves around policy issues, such as how to balance the need to ensure that recycling occurs nationwide as well as industry's interests in a uniform, national approach with states' prerogatives to tailor used electronics management toward their individual needs and preferences. In the end, these larger policy issues are matters for negotiation among the concerned parties and for decision making by Congress and the administration.

At the same time, there are a number of beneficial actions that the federal government is already taking that, as currently devised, do not require the effort and implications of new legislation, but rather would complement any of the broader strategies that policymakers might ultimately endorse. In particular, EPA's collaborative efforts—including Plug-In To eCycling, the R2 practices, EPEAT, and the Federal Electronics Challenge—have demonstrated considerable potential and, in some cases, quantifiable benefits. However, these programs' achievements have been limited or uncertain, and EPA has not systematically analyzed the programs to determine whether their impact could be augmented. Moreover, EPA has not developed an integrated strategy that articulates how the programs, taken together, can best assist stakeholders to achieve the environmentally responsible management of used electronics.

A key issue of national significance to the management of used electronics is how to address exports—an issue that, according to many stakeholders, would most appropriately be addressed at the federal level. EPA has taken useful steps by developing a legislative package for ratification of the Basel Convention, as we recommended in 2008. However, EPA has not yet worked with other agencies, including the State Department and the Council on Environmental Quality, to finalize a proposal for the administration to provide to Congress for review and consideration. While there are unresolved issues regarding the environmentally sound management of used electronics under the Basel Convention, providing Congress with a legislative package for ratification could provide a basis for further deliberation and, perhaps, resolution of such issues.

Recommendations for Executive Action

We recommend that the Administrator of EPA undertake an examination of the agency's partnership programs for the management of used electronics. The analysis should examine how the impacts of such programs can be augmented, and should culminate in an integrated strategy that articulates how the programs, taken together, can best assist stakeholders in achieving the environmentally responsible management of used electronics nationwide.

In addition, we recommend that the Administrator of EPA work with other federal agencies, including the State Department and the Council on Environmental Quality, to finalize a legislative proposal that would be needed for ratification of the Basel Convention, with the aim of submitting a package for congressional consideration.

AGENCY COMMENTS AND OUR EVALUATION

We provided a draft of this report to EPA for review and comment.. EPA agreed with both of our recommendations and also provided additional clarifications and editorial suggestions, which we have incorporated into the report as appropriate.

Regarding our recommendation for an examination of the agency's partnership programs culminating in an integrated strategy for the management of used electronics, EPA stated that the agency plans to gather and analyze input from a variety of stakeholders and to incorporate the input into such a strategy. In addition, while pointing out that the agency's partnership programs already reflect an integrated approach, in that they address the full life cycle of electronic products, from design through end-of-life management, EPA acknowledged that the programs can and should be augmented and stated that the agency is committed to doing so within the limits of declining resources. In particular, EPA outlined a number of potential efforts to improve the environmental attributes of electronics, increase collection and the appropriate management of used electronics, and better control exports. EPA also stated that the agency is considering the need for new legislative and regulatory authority. We acknowledge EPA's progress in developing partnership programs to address the full life cycle of electronic products but continue to emphasize the need for a comprehensive, written strategy that addresses how the programs can best promote the environmentally sound management of used electronics. Such a document has the potential to help coordinate the efforts of the many stakeholders associated with the management of used electronics to further promote their environmentally sound reuse and recycling, and to more effectively communicate the strategy to Congress and other decision makers.

Regarding our recommendation that EPA work with other federal agencies to finalize a legislative proposal needed to ratify the Basel

Convention, EPA commented that the agency has already begun working with the State Department and other federal agencies to do so. EPA added that its previous work in developing such a legislative proposal should enable it to successfully complete this effort. We acknowledge this work but point out that Congress will only have the opportunity to deliberate on a tangible proposal if the effort to achieve consensus on an administration-approved position on the matter is accorded the priority needed.

Sincerely yours,
John B. Stephenson
Director, Natural Resources and Environment

APPENDIX I: SCOPE AND METHODOLOGY

To examine the Environmental Protection Agency's (EPA) efforts to facilitate the environmentally sound management of used electronics, we reviewed solid and hazardous waste laws and regulations—including the Resource Conservation and Recovery Act and EPA's rule on the management of cathode-ray tubes (CRT)—and their applicability to used electronics. We specifically reviewed EPA documents describing the agency's efforts to enforce the CRT rule and to address concerns raised in our August 2008 report on electronic waste exports, including information on the number of EPA investigations of possible violations of the CRT rule.[1] We also examined publicly available information on specific enforcement actions against companies, companies approved to export CRTs for recycling, and companies that have submitted notifications of exports for reuse, and we obtained aggregate information from EPA on its enforcement efforts. To obtain EPA's views on its efforts, we interviewed officials from the agency's Office of Enforcement and Compliance Assurance and the Office of Solid Waste and Emergency Response. To examine EPA's promotion of partnership programs, we interviewed EPA officials responsible for implementing or representing the agency's position on Plug-In To eCycling, the Responsible Recycling (R2) practices, and the Electronic Product Environmental Assessment Tool (EPEAT). In addition, we interviewed stakeholders concerned about the management of used electronics—including environmental groups; state and local government officials; and electronics manufacturers, retailers, and recyclers—to obtain their views on EPA's efforts.

To examine the views of manufacturers, retailers, recyclers, state and local governments, and other stakeholders on the state-by-state approach to the management of used electronics, we conducted a broad range of interviews. For each category of stakeholders, we conducted interviews with key national-level organizations or associations with a broad perspective on the management of used electronics across the United States and reviewed any related policy positions or reports. To gain further insights, we interviewed individual stakeholders in each category of stakeholders, including state and local government officials and other stakeholders, in five states with electronics recycling legislation that we selected for detailed review—California, Maine, Minnesota, Texas, and Washington. To supplement these detailed reviews, we interviewed state and local government officials in three states without legislation—Arizona, Florida, and New Hampshire. For each interview, we generally discussed the collection and recycling rates for used electronics, the convenience of collection opportunities to consumers, efforts to ensure environmentally sound management, and the impact of the state-by-state approach on implementation of state electronics recycling legislation and on stakeholders' compliance or enforcement efforts. While recognizing that stakeholders may benefit from state legislation, such as through an increase in business opportunities for electronics recyclers, we specifically asked about the burden (if any) created by the state-by-state approach. For the five states with electronics recycling legislation, we reviewed the laws and related regulations, as well as other documents on the implementation and outcomes of the law, and we visited the states to conduct in-person interviews.

We encountered a number of limitations in the availability of reliable data on the impact of the state-by-state approach on various stakeholders. For example, the five states we selected did not have data on collection and recycling rates prior to the effective dates of their laws, which would be useful to quantify the impact of their programs. Similarly, some manufacturers and other stakeholders regulated under state laws had concerns about providing proprietary information or did not identify compliance costs in a way that enabled us to determine the portion of costs that stems from having to comply with differing state requirements. Due to such limitations, we relied predominately on stakeholders' statements regarding how they have been impacted under the state-bystate approach. Additional information on the stakeholders we interviewed includes the following:

- *State and local government officials.* For a national perspective, we interviewed representatives of the Association of State and Territorial

Solid Waste Management Officials, the Eastern Regional Conference of the Council of State Governments, the National Conference of State Legislatures, and the National Governors Association. For the five states with electronics recycling legislation we selected for detailed review, we interviewed state legislators or legislative staff involved in enacting the laws, state environmental agency officials responsible for implementing the laws, and local solid waste management officials. We selected the five states to ensure coverage of the two basic models of state electronics recycling legislation, a recycling fee paid by consumers and producer responsibility, as well as the variations of the producer responsibility model. In addition, we selected states with recycling programs that had been in place long enough for stakeholders to provide an assessment of the impacts of the legislation. For the three states without electronics recycling legislation we selected for detailed review, we conducted telephone interviews with state and local solid waste management officials and (in Arizona and New Hampshire) legislators who have introduced legislation or been active in studying options for the management of used electronics. We selected the three states to include ones that, in part, had addressed the management of certain used electronics through other means, such as a ban on landfill disposal or grants for voluntary recycling efforts, and to ensure variety in terms of location and size.

- Electronics manufacturers. For a broad perspective, we interviewed representatives of two national associations of electronics manufacturers: the Consumer Electronics Association and the Information Technology Industry Council. We also interviewed representatives of a judgmental sample of nine individual manufacturers. We selected manufacturers to interview to include a range of sizes and business models, including manufacturers of information technology equipment and televisions as well as companies that no longer manufacture products covered under state laws but still bear responsibility for recycling costs in some states. In addition to these interviews, we reviewed manufacturers' policy positions and other documents on the state-by-state approach to managing used electronics or on particular state and local electronics recycling legislation.
- Electronics retailers. We interviewed representatives of the Consumer Electronics Retailers Coalition, an association of consumer electronics

retailers, and of a judgmental sample of four national consumer electronics retailers, including retailers that are also considered manufacturers or collectors under some state electronics recycling legislation. In each of the five states we selected for detailed review, we spoke with representatives from state retail associations, whose members include large national retailers, as well as smaller retailers operating in the five states. We also reviewed available documents pertaining to retailers' efforts in managing used electronics and their policy positions on the state-by-state approach.

- Recyclers and refurbishers of used electronics. For a broad perspective from the electronics recycling industry, we interviewed a representative of the Institute of Scrap Recycling Industries, many of whose members are involved in the recycling of used electronics. In addition, for the perspective of refurbishers, we conducted an interview with TechSoup, a nonprofit organization that has established a partnership with Microsoft to increase the number of personal computers available to nonprofits, schools, and low-income families across the globe by reducing the cost of software to refurbishers. We also interviewed representatives of a judgmental sample of recyclers and refurbishers encompassing a variety of sizes and business models, including large corporations operating in multiple states as well as nonprofit organizations or smaller entities operating in a single state. In particular, in each of the five states with electronics recycling legislation we selected for detailed review, we interviewed at least one recycler operating under the state program and one refurbisher.
- *Environmental and other nonprofit organizations*. We interviewed representatives of environmental and other nonprofit organizations that have an interest in the issue of the management of used electronics, including the Basel Action Network, Consumers Union, Electronics TakeBack Coalition, Product Stewardship Institute, and Silicon Valley Toxics Coalition. In addition, in the five states with electronics recycling legislation we selected for detailed review, we interviewed representatives of state environmental organizations that advocated for the state legislation or have been active in tracking the implementation of the laws. For each of the environmental and nonprofit organizations interviewed, we reviewed available documents pertaining to their advocacy work and their views on the

state-by-state approach or particular state electronics recycling legislation.

To examine the implications of alternative national strategies to further promote the environmentally sound management of used electronics, we reviewed relevant existing laws relating to solid and hazardous waste management (the Resource Conservation and Recovery Act and the Mercury-Containing and Rechargeable Battery Management Act). In addition, we examined state laws establishing electronics recycling programs or addressing the management of used electronics through other means, such as a ban on landfill disposal, to identify components of the laws that might be addressed under a national approach. We also examined the European Union's directive on waste electrical and electronic equipment and electronics recycling in Canada as examples of how used electronics are managed internationally. As part of our interviews with national-level organizations or associations of stakeholders, as well as with individual stakeholders, we discussed stakeholder efforts to coordinate state electronics recycling programs and stakeholders' policy positions on a national strategy, including their views on the components of a national strategy, such as a mechanism for financing the cost of recycling. Regarding alternative strategies specifically relating to exports of used electronics, we examined ways that state electronics recycling programs we selected for detailed review had addressed the issue, and we interviewed stakeholders regarding current state and EPA efforts to limit potentially harmful exports.

We also reviewed EPA documents and interviewed EPA officials regarding the statutory changes necessary for the United States to ratify the Basel Convention on the Control of Transboundary Movements of Hazardous Wastes and Their Disposal, as well as the implications of ratification on the agency's ability to exercise greater oversight over the export of used electronics for reuse or recycling. Finally, we reviewed EPA's technical assistance comments on a congressional concept paper proposing a framework for establishing a national electronics recycling program.

We conducted this performance audit from May 2009 to July 2010 in accordance with generally accepted government auditing standards. Those standards require that we plan and perform the audit to obtain sufficient, appropriate evidence to provide a reasonable basis for our findings and conclusions based on our audit objectives. We believe that the evidence obtained provides a reasonable basis for our findings and conclusions based on our audit objectives.

APPENDIX II: STATE ELECTRONICS RECYCLING PROGRAMS

The five states with electronics recycling laws that we selected for detailed review—California, Maine, Minnesota, Texas, and Washington— illustrate a range of ways of addressing elements and issues common to the management of used electronics.[1] For each of the states, we describe three key elements we identified as establishing the framework for their recycling programs: (1) the mechanism for financing the cost of collecting and recycling used electronics, (2) the mechanism for providing for the convenient collection of used electronics, and (3) requirements for the environmentally sound management of used electronics collected under the programs and the state's enforcement of the requirements. In addition, because the state electronics recycling programs are relatively new, we describe developments and program changes designed to address issues encountered during the initial implementation of the programs.

California

California's electronics recycling law established a funding mechanism to provide for the collection and recycling of certain video display devices that have a screen greater than 4 inches, measured diagonally, and that are identified by the state Department of Toxic Substances Control as a hazardous waste when discarded.[2] According to state officials, the state's list of covered devices currently includes computer monitors, laptop computers, portable DVD players, and most televisions.

Financing Mechanism

California is the only state identified as having an electronics recycling law that established a system to finance collection and recycling costs through a recycling fee paid by consumers. Effective on January 1, 2005, retailers began collecting the fee at the time of purchase of certain video display devices. The fee currently ranges from $8 to $25, depending on screen size. Retailers remit the fees to the state, and they may retain 3 percent as reimbursement for costs associated with collection of the fee. The state, in turn, uses the fees to reimburse collectors and recyclers of covered electronic devices as well as for administering and educating the public about the program. Entities must be approved by the state to be eligible to receive collection and recycling payments. There were about 600 approved collectors and 60 approved recyclers as of October 2009. To determine the amount paid per pound, the state periodically updates information concerning the net costs of collection and recycling and adjusts the statewide payment rates. To assist the state in this effort, approved collectors and recyclers are required to submit annual reports on their net collection and recycling costs for the prior year. As of May 2010, the combined statewide rate for collection and recycling was $0.39 per pound. The administration of the program is shared by three state agencies. The State Board of Equalization is responsible for collecting the fee from and auditing retailers. The Department of Resources Recycling and Recovery (CalRecycle) has overall responsibility for administering collection and recycling payments. Specific duties of CalRecycle include establishing the collection and recycling payment schedule to cover the net costs of authorized collectors and recyclers; approving applications to become an approved collector or recycler; reviewing recycling payment claims for the appropriate collection, transfer, and processing documentation and making payments; and addressing any identified fraud in payment claims. Under the law, CalRecycle is also responsible for reviewing the fee paid by consumers at least once every 2 years and adjusting the fee to ensure sufficient revenues to fund the recycling program. The third agency, the Department of Toxic Substances Control, is responsible for determining whether a video display device, when discarded or disposed of, is presumed to be a hazardous waste under the state health and safety code and, therefore, is a covered electronic device under the electronics recycling legislation. In addition, the department regulates the management of used electronics and conducts annual inspections of recyclers to ensure compliance with applicable laws and regulations.

Mechanism for Providing Collection Opportunities

One of the purposes of the California law was to establish a program that is "cost free and convenient" for consumers to return and recycle used electronics generated in the state. To this end, the law directs the state to establish a payment schedule that covers the net cost for authorized collectors to operate a free and convenient system for collection, consolidation, and transportation. State and local government officials, as well as other state stakeholders we interviewed, told us the law has resulted in convenient collection opportunities. For example, a representative of the state's Regional Council of Rural Counties said that, while it does not require counties to provide collection opportunities, the law had resulted in convenient collection in rural counties. Similarly, according to Sacramento County solid waste management officials, the law has made it profitable for the private sector to collect and recycle used electronics and thereby has freed up county resources to pay for media campaigns to inform the public about the law and to offer curbside collection.

Requirements for Environmentally Sound Management

Recyclers approved under the state's payment system for the recycling of covered electronic devices must be inspected at least once annually by the Department of Toxic Substances Control and be found in conformance with the department's regulations to maintain their approval. The department's regulations restrict certain recycling activities—such as using water, chemicals, or external heat to disassemble electronic devices—and specify requirements in a variety of other areas, including training of personnel, record-keeping, and the labeling of containers. In addition, to be eligible for a claim within the payment system, covered devices must be dismantled in California and the residuals generally must be sent to appropriate recycling facilities. Hence, the program does not pay claims for any covered devices that are exported intact. The state's electronics recycling legislation also requires that exporters notify the department and demonstrate that the covered electronic waste or covered electronic devices are being exported for the purposes of recycling or disposal; that the importation of the waste or device is not prohibited by an applicable law in the country of destination; and that the waste or device will be managed only at facilities whose operations meet certain standards for environmentally sound management. (These demonstrations are not required for exports of a component part of a covered electronic device that is exported to an authorized collector or recycler and that is reused or recycled into a new electronic component.) According to a department official responsible for implementing the regulations, the state's ability to withhold payment for the recycling of covered electronic devices is an effective tool for promoting compliance with the regulations. However, the official also said that the state lacks the authority to regulate exports (e.g., exports of CRT glass containing lead for processing in Mexico, which, according to the official, does not have regulations equivalent to those in California).

Developments Since the Law's Implementation

Key developments since the initiation of California's program in 2005 include the following adjustments to the recycling fee paid by consumers and to the payment schedule for collection and recycling:

- Effective January 2009, CalRecycle increased the recycling fee from an initial range of $6 to $10 to the current range of $8 to $25. As described in the CalRecycle's January 2008 update on the program, a continued growth in the volume of recycling payment claims resulted in the pace of payments exceeding the flow of revenue generated by the fee. CalRecycle adjusted the fee to avoid exhausting the fund used to pay for the collection and recycling of used electronics.
- In 2008, CalRecycle decreased the payment schedule for combined collection and recycling. The initial rate was $0.48 per pound, based in part on a provisional rate established by the law, and the current rate is $0.39 per pound. According to CalRecycle officials, the initial payment schedule was artificially high, which benefited the program by fostering a recycling infrastructure in the state. CalRecycle adjusted the payment schedule on the basis of an analysis of the net cost reports submitted by collectors and recyclers.

MAINE

Maine's electronics recycling program began in 2006 and finances the cost of recycling televisions, computers, computer monitors, digital picture frames, printers, and video game consoles from households.[3]

Financing Mechanism

Maine's law is based on the concept of "shared responsibility," whereby participating municipalities generally bear the costs associated with collection and manufacturers finance handling and recycling costs associated with managing certain used electronics generated by households. Participating municipalities arrange for these used electronics to be transported to state-approved consolidators, which count and weigh information technology products by brand and manufacturer and determine the total weight of televisions and video game consoles. Consolidators who are also recyclers may then further process the used electronics; otherwise, they send the material to recycling facilities.[4] In either case, consolidators generally invoice individual manufacturers for their handling, transportation, and recycling costs. The state approves each consolidator's fee schedule, currently set at a maximum of $0.48 per pound for combined recovery and recycling, for use when invoicing manufacturers. For information technology products, the amount invoiced is based on the weight of the manufacturer's own brand of electronics collected under the program (return share) plus a proportional share of products for which the manufacturer cannot be identified or is no longer in business (orphan share). In contrast, for manufacturers of televisions and video game consoles with a national market share that exceeds a certain minimum threshold, the amount invoiced is calculated as the total weight collected multiplied by the proportion of the manufacturer's national market share of sales for those products (recycling share). Initially, Maine's law only used return share as a basis for determining the financial responsibility of all manufacturers. The state amended the law in 2009 to base the financial responsibility of television manufacturers (as well as video game consoles) on market share. The Maine Department of Environmental Protection had recommended this change in part to address the issue of the relatively long lifespan of televisions and the concern among long-standing television manufacturers that, under the return share system, new market entrants do not bear recycling costs and can therefore offer their products at a lower price and possibly even go out of business before their products enter the waste stream.

The Department of Environmental Protection has overall responsibility for the electronics recycling program. The department's responsibilities include approving consolidators as well as the fee schedule used by consolidators in charging manufacturers, determining the orphan share for manufacturers of information technology products, and determining the recycling share for manufacturers of televisions and video game consoles on the basis of national sales data. In addition, the department is responsible for enforcing the compliance of manufacturers whose products are sold in the state. Finally, the department notifies retailers of noncompliant manufacturers (retailers are prohibited from selling products of such manufacturers).

Mechanism for Providing Collection Opportunities

One of the purposes of Maine's law is to establish a recycling system that is convenient and minimizes the cost to consumers of electronic products and components. In addition, manufacturers are responsible for paying the reasonable operational costs of consolidators, including the costs associated with ensuring that consolidation facilities are geographically located to conveniently serve all areas of the state as determined by the Department of Environmental Protection. To establish convenient collection opportunities for households, Maine's program relies on the state's existing municipal waste collection infrastructure and provides an incentive to municipalities to participate by giving them access to essentially free recycling of certain covered electronics. The law allows participating municipalities to collect used electronics at a local or regional waste transfer station or recycling facility or through other means, such as curbside pickup. According to a 2007 survey supported by the department, most municipalities provide permanent collection sites. About half of the municipalities that responded to the survey reported that they charge end-of-life fees for accepting used electronics from households to offset the costs associated with collection. However, local solid waste management officials we interviewed also told us that the program implemented under the law enabled municipalities to reduce or eliminate fees. For example, the Portland solid waste manager said that the program enabled the city to stop charging residents a fee, which was approximately $20 per television or computer monitor prior to the law. Notably, Maine law now prohibits the disposal of CRTs in landfills and other solid waste disposal facilities.

Requirements for Environmentally Sound Management

Maine's law requires that recyclers provide to consolidators a sworn certification that they meet guidelines for environmentally sound management published by the Department of Environmental Protection. Among other things, the guidelines stipulate that recyclers comply with federal, state, and local laws and regulations relevant to the handling, processing, refurbishment, and recycling of used electronics; implement training and other measures to safeguard occupational and environmental health and safety; and comply with federal and international law and agreements regarding the export of used products or materials. Other guidelines specific to exports include a requirement that televisions and computer monitors destined for reuse include only whole products that have been tested and certified as being in working order or as requiring only minor repair, and where the recipient has verified a market for the sale or donation of the equipment.

The Department of Environmental Protection official in charge of the program told us she has visited the facilities that recycle used electronics collected under Maine's program, but that the department lacks the resources and auditing expertise to ensure adherence to the guidelines as well as the authority to audit out-of-state recyclers.

Developments Since the Law's Implementation

Since Maine initiated its electronics recycling program, the state made a number of changes to the law, and the Department of Environmental Protection has suggested additional changes. Such changes include the following:

- *Scope of covered electronic devices.* In 2009, Maine added several products, including digital picture frames and printers, to the scope of covered devices. In its 2008 report on the recycling program, the Department of Environmental Protection had recommended adding digital picture frames and printers for a number of reasons, including the growing volume of such equipment in the waste stream. In its 2010 report, the department also recommended the program be expanded to include used electronics generated by small businesses, thereby increasing the volume of used electronics collected, providing for more efficient transportation from collection sites, and providing for a greater volume to recyclers as a means to drive down the per-pound cost of recycling.
- *Program administration.* Beginning in July 2010, manufacturers of covered devices sold in the state are required to pay an annual registration fee of $3,000 to offset the state's administrative costs associated with the program. In its January 2010 report, the Department of Environmental Protection recommended that the state legislature consider eliminating or reducing the fee for certain manufacturers, such as small television manufacturers. According to the report, an exemption from paying the fee would provide relief to

manufacturers that no longer sell or have not sold significant quantities of covered devices in the state.

- *Recycling costs.* In its January 2010 report, the Department of Environmental Protection noted that, while direct comparisons between differing state programs are difficult, recycling costs are higher in Maine than in other states with electronics recycling laws. Representatives of both the Consumer Electronics Association and the Information Technology Industry Council also told us that recycling costs in Maine are higher because the state selects consolidators and approves the fee schedule used by each of the consolidators to invoice manufacturers, thereby limiting competition. To address such concerns, the department stated its intent to take a number of administrative actions. For example, the department plans to streamline the permitting process for facilities that process used electronics and thereby encourage the growth of recycling facilities in the state and reduce the handling and shipping costs for used electronics, much of which is currently processed out of state. The department also plans to examine ways to increase the competitiveness of the cost approval process for consolidators or price limits that can be imposed without compromising the level of service currently afforded to municipalities.

Minnesota

Minnesota initiated its program in 2007 to finance the recycling of certain used electronics from households.[5] Manufacturers of video display devices (televisions, computer monitors, and laptop computers) with a screen size that is greater than 9 inches, measured diagonally, that are sold in the state are responsible for recycling, including costs, and can also meet their obligations by financing the recycling of printers, keyboards, DVD players, and certain other electronics.

Financing Mechanism

Minnesota's law establishes recycling targets for manufacturers selling video display devices in the state. The targets are set at an amount of used electronics equal to 80 percent of the weight of video display devices sold to households during the year. (The target was 60 percent for the first program year.) Manufacturers that exceed their targets earn recycling credits that can be used to meet their targets in subsequent years or sold to other manufacturers. Conversely, manufacturers that fail to meet their targets pay recycling fees on the basis of how close they are toward meeting their obligation. State officials told us the recycling program is based primarily on market economics and does not require significant government involvement. In particular, the state does not set the prices paid for recycling, and manufacturers have flexibility in selecting collectors and recyclers to work with. Recyclers seek to be reimbursed for their costs by marketing and selling recycling pounds to manufacturers. According to several stakeholders we interviewed about the state's program, this market-based approach has contributed to lowering recycling costs in the state.

The Minnesota Pollution Control Agency has primary responsibility for administering the program. The agency's responsibilities include reviewing registrations submitted by manufacturers for completeness; maintaining registrations submitted by collectors and recyclers; and conducting educational outreach efforts regarding the program. The state department of revenue reviews manufacturers' annual registration fees and reports and, among other things, collects data needed to support manufacturers' fee determinations. The state uses registration fees to cover the cost of implementing the program, which may include awarding grants to entities that provide collection and recycling services. The Minnesota Pollution Control Agency has requested proposals to provide grants for collection and recycling outside of the Minneapolis-St. Paul metropolitan area and expects to award several grants in 2010.

Mechanism for Providing Collection Opportunities

Minnesota's law does not stipulate criteria for the establishment of a statewide collection infrastructure or mandate that any entity serve as a collector, but rather relies on the reimbursement from manufacturers to create an incentive for the establishment of collection opportunities. To foster the availability of collection opportunities outside of the Minneapolis-St. Paul metropolitan area, the law allows 11/2 times the weight of covered electronic devices collected outside of the metropolitan area to count toward manufacturers' recycling targets. Local solid waste management officials we interviewed described the impact of the state's electronics recycling legislation on the convenience of collection opportunities as dependent upon whether a county already had an established recycling program for used electronics, with a greater impact in counties that did not already have recycling programs.

Requirements for Environmentally Sound Management

Minnesota's law prohibits the commercial use of prison labor to recycle video display devices and requires that recyclers abide by relevant federal, state, and local regulations and carry liability insurance for environmental releases, accidents, and other emergencies. The law does not establish additional requirements for environmentally sound management. In addition, Minnesota Pollution Control Agency officials said that they have limited resources to ensure that used electronics are managed responsibly, particularly when equipment is shipped out of state, and that enforcement efforts are largely based on self-policing by recyclers and spot checks of larger recyclers. Two recyclers in the state with whom we spoke said that a lack of oversight of recyclers by state authorities had contributed to undercutting by irresponsible recyclers. Minnesota Pollution Control Agency officials said they are seeking to promote certification programs, such as R2 or e-Stewards®, for electronics recyclers operating in the state.

Developments Since the Law's Implementation

Minnesota amended its law in 2009 to make the following changes:

- The state amended the law to remove the requirement that retailers annually report to each video display device manufacturer the number of the manufacturer's brand of video display devices sold to households during the previous year. Manufacturers submitted this information to the state, which used it to determine manufacturers' recycling targets. A representative of the Minnesota Retailers Association said that retailers found this requirement to be a burden. Similarly, according to the Consumer Electronics Retailers Coalition, the state's reporting requirement imposed a high cost on retailers and increased the risk of the disclosure of proprietary sales data. Minnesota now uses either manufacturer-provided data or national sales data, prorated to the state's population, to determine manufacturers' obligations.

- The state further amended the law to limit the use of recycling credits. Minnesota Pollution Control Agency officials told us this amendment was intended to address a "boom and bust" scenario, whereby manufacturers financed the recycling of large amounts of used electronics in the first program year and accumulated carry-over credits, which they used to meet their recycling targets during the second year. The use of credits left local governments and electronics recyclers responsible for the cost of collecting and recycling used electronics that exceeded manufacturers' recycling targets. As a result, according to local solid waste management officials we interviewed, some counties reintroduced end-of-life fees and saw an increase in the illegal dumping of used electronics. To address such issues and ensure that a majority of targets are met by the recycling of newly collected material, the amended law limits the portion of a manufacturer's target that can be met through carry-over credits to 25 percent. Prior to the amendment, the law did not limit the use of recycling credits.

Since the implementation of Minnesota's program, several other states, including Illinois[6] and Wisconsin,[7] have incorporated the use of recycling targets into electronics recycling legislation. Several stakeholders told us they prefer targets as they are designed in the Illinois program. For example, a representative of one electronics manufacturer said he expects that manufacturers will have difficulty in meeting their targets in Minnesota in upcoming years after recyclers have worked through the backlog of used electronics stored in consumers' homes prior to implementation of the state's law.

In contrast, under the Illinois program, manufacturers' targets are based in part on the total amount recycled or reused during the prior year, such that the targets may be adjusted downward if the amounts collected decrease. Similarly, several refurbishers of used electronics pointed out that Minnesota's law does not allow the refurbishment of covered electronic devices to count toward manufacturers' recycling targets and thereby, according to some stakeholders, may create an incentive to recycle equipment that has been collected but is in working condition or can be refurbished. In contrast, under Illinois' law, the weight of covered electronic devices processed for reuse is doubled when determining whether a manufacturer has met its recycling and reuse target, and the weight is tripled if the refurbished equipment is donated to a public school or nonprofit entity.

TEXAS

Texas' computer equipment recycling program began in 2008 and requires manufacturers to provide opportunities for free collection of desktop and laptop computers, monitors not containing a tuner, and accompanying mice and keyboards from consumers in the state.[8] Consumers are defined as individuals who use computer equipment purchased primarily for personal or home-business use.

Financing Mechanism

Texas' computer equipment recycling law is based on the concept of "individual producer responsibility," whereby manufacturers of computer equipment are responsible for implementing a recovery plan for collecting their own brand of used equipment from consumers. The state's program requires that each manufacturer submit its plan to the state and annually report the weight of computer equipment collected, recycled, and reused. The law does not authorize manufacturer registration fees, and manufacturers are free to select the recyclers with whom they work and negotiate recycling rates to be paid.

The Texas Commission on Environmental Quality has the primary responsibility for enforcing the law. The commission's responsibilities include providing information on the Internet about manufacturers' recovery plans; educating consumers regarding the collection, recycling, and reuse of computer equipment; helping to ensure that electronics retailers do not sell the equipment of manufacturers without recovery plans; and annually compiling information submitted by manufacturers and issuing a report to the state legislature. According to commission officials, manufacturers not paying registration fees has not caused a financial burden because the commission already had the expertise and outreach capabilities needed to implement the law.

Mechanism for Providing Collection Opportunities

The Texas law requires that the collection of computer equipment be reasonably convenient and available to consumers in the state. In addition, manufacturers' recovery plans must enable consumers to recycle computer equipment without paying a separate fee at the time of recycling. The law allows manufacturers to fulfill these requirements by offering a system for returning computer equipment by mail, establishing a physical collection site, or organizing a collection event or by offering some combination of these or other options. According to Texas Commission on Environmental Quality officials, most manufacturers have opted to offer a mail-back program, and one manufacturer noted that the mail-back programs may be more convenient for rural residents of the state than a physical collection point. Some manufacturers have provided additional collection options. For example, in addition to providing a mail-back option, Dell has partnered with affiliates of Goodwill Industries in the state to establish a physical collection infrastructure.

The local solid waste management officials we interviewed regarding the state's computer equipment recycling law were critical of the impact of the law on providing collection opportunities and relieving local governments of the burden of managing used electronics. These officials attributed the law's lack of impact to a number of factors, including the inconvenience to consumers of manufacturers' mail-back programs; insufficient education of consumers about recycling opportunities by manufacturers, the Texas Commission on Environmental Quality, or local governments; and manufacturers having responsibility only for the cost of recycling computer equipment collected directly from consumers, not for that collected by local governments (e.g., when consumers may be unaware of the opportunities for free recycling). As a result, while they are not required to collect used computer equipment, local governments bear the costs for the equipment they collect.

For example, the solid waste coordinator for one regional council of governments said that the council continues to provide grants to local governments for the management of used electronics.

Requirements for Environmentally Sound Management

The Texas electronics recycling law requires that computer equipment collected under the law be recycled or reused in a manner that complies with federal, state, and local law.

In addition, the law directed the Texas Commission on Environmental Quality to adopt standards for the management of used electronics developed by the Institute for Scrap Recycling Industries, which represents electronics recyclers, or to adopt such standards from a comparable organization.

Among other things, the standards adopted by the commission require that recyclers prioritize refurbishment over recycling and recycling over disposal, ensure that computer equipment is stored and processed in a manner that minimizes the potential release of any hazardous substance into the environment, and have a written plan for responding to and reporting pollutant releases. Manufacturers are required to certify that recyclers have followed the standards in recycling the manufacturers' computer equipment.

Texas Commission on Environmental Quality officials said that, under the commission's risk-based approach to enforcement of environmental regulations, they had not prioritized regular, scheduled enforcement of the requirements for the environmentally sound management of used computer equipment collected under the state's program.

They said that they would follow up on any allegations of noncompliance with the requirements, but that they had not received any such complaints. Several recyclers in the state confirmed that there had been minimal oversight of recyclers by the commission and said that manufacturers play a more active role than the commission in ensuring that the recyclers with whom they contract adhere to requirements for environmentally sound management.

Developments Since the Law's Implementation

In 2009, the Texas state legislature passed a bill that would have required that television manufacturers collect and recycle an amount of televisions on the basis of manufacturers' market share of equipment sold in the state. However, the bill was vetoed by the governor, who stated that it was significantly different than the law covering computer equipment—for example, in that the bill would impose fees on television manufacturers and recyclers.

Local solid waste management officials we interviewed, as well as a state environmental group that focuses on used electronics, were critical of the governor's veto.

For example, according to the environmental group, the bill would have relieved local governments of the costs associated with managing used televisions, and without a law establishing a recycling program, televisions will continue to be disposed of in landfills, which is not prohibited in Texas.

WASHINGTON

Washington's electronics recycling law was passed in 2006, and the program began full operation in 2009.[9] The program covers the costs associated with collecting, transporting, and processing desktop and laptop computers, computer monitors, and televisions generated by households, charities, school districts, small businesses with fewer than 50 employees, and small governments (cities with a population of fewer than 50,000, counties with a population fewer than 125,000, and special purpose districts).

Financing Mechanism

Under Washington's law, manufacturers are required to finance the collection, transportation, and recycling of certain used electronics. The law allows manufacturers to meet this requirement by implementing an independent, state-approved collection and recycling plan or by participating in the default "standard plan." In addition, the law requires that individual manufacturers register with the Department of Ecology, the state agency responsible for administering the law, and pay a fee to cover the department's administrative costs. The fees are based on a sliding scale linked to a manufacturer's annual sales of covered electronic products in the state. The specific responsibilities of the department include reviewing the standard plan as well as any independent plans submitted by manufacturers for the department's approval; establishing an annual process for local governments and local communities to report their satisfaction with the services provided by the plans; registering manufacturers, collectors, transporters, and processors for the program; and enforcing the law (e.g., by issuing warnings and penalties against manufacturers selling covered products in the state if they are not participating in an approved plan).

The standard plan is implemented by the Washington Materials Management and Financing Authority, a public body created by the state's law. All manufacturers are required to be members of the authority and the standard plan, or they can opt out of the standard plan by gaining the state's approval for their own independent plan. Currently, all manufacturers affected by the state's law meet their requirements through participation in the standard plan. The Washington Materials Management and Financing Authority assesses individual manufacturers for collection and recycling costs, as well as the authority's administrative costs, on the basis of a combination of market share and return share, with the return share being based on an annual sampling of used electronics collected under the state's program. The authority uses the assessments paid by manufacturers to reimburse individual collectors, transporters, and recyclers at rates negotiated with the authority. According to the director of the authority, the combined rate for the collection, transportation, and recycling of used electronics, as well as administrative costs, was $0.24 per pound in 2009. A number of stakeholders noted that the authority has the ability to negotiate relatively low prices, in comparison with some other state electronics recycling programs, due to the authority's purchasing power over electronics recycling services in the state.

Mechanism for Providing Collection Opportunities

Washington's electronics recycling law includes a number of specific requirements for the establishment of a convenient collection network throughout the state, in both urban and rural areas. In particular, the law requires that each plan provide collection service in every county and every city or town with a population greater than 10,000. Collection sites may include electronics recyclers and repair shops, recyclers of other commodities, reuse organizations, charities, retailers, government recycling sites, or other locations. Plans may limit the number of used electronics accepted per customer per day or per delivery at a collection site or service but are also required to provide free processing of large quantities of used electronics generated by small businesses, small governments, charities, and school districts.

Local solid waste management officials told us the law has had a positive impact on promoting the collection of used electronics in the state. One of these officials also said that the law's implementation has eliminated the cost burden on local government for managing used electronics. In contrast, representatives of several manufacturers, as well as the Consumer Electronics Association, told us that the law's requirements for convenience are too prescriptive and have served as an impediment for manufacturers to obtain approval for their independent plans. Along these lines, in 2009, the Department of Ecology rejected two independent plans submitted by manufacturers because the department concluded that the plans did not meet the law's convenience criteria. Department officials told us they expect the plans to be resubmitted and approved once the manufacturers submitting the plans demonstrated that they would be able to meet the convenience criteria.

Requirements for Environmentally Sound Management

The Department of Ecology established both minimum standards and voluntary "preferred" standards for the environmentally sound management of used electronics. Among other things, the minimum standards require that recyclers implement an environmental, health, and safety management system; remove any parts that contain materials of concern, such as devices containing mercury, prior to mechanical or thermal processing and handle them in a manner consistent with the regulatory requirements that apply to the items; and not use prison labor for the recycling of used electronics.

The department encourages recyclers to conform to the preferred standards and identifies recyclers that do so on its Web site. In addition, the Washington Materials Management and Financing Authority made the preferred standards a requirement for all recyclers with whom the authority contracts under the standard plan. Among other things, the preferred standards stipulate that recyclers use only downstream vendors that adhere to both the minimum and voluntary standards with respect to materials of concern; ensure that recipient countries legally accept exports of materials of concern; and, as with the minimum standards, undergo an annual audit of the recycler's conformance with the standards.

Department of Ecology officials said that the authority's requirement that recyclers achieve preferred status had enabled the authority to achieve more than what the state could legally require, particularly regarding exports.

Developments Since the Law's Implementation

Washington amended its law in 2009 to authorize collectors in receipt of fully functioning computers to sell or donate them as whole products for reuse. The amendment requires that collectors not include computers gleaned for reuse when seeking compensation under a standard or independent plan. In addition, when taking parts from computers submitted for compensation (i.e., for recycling) to repair other computers for reuse, collectors must make a part-for-part exchange with the nonfunctioning computers submitted for compensation.

According to Department of Ecology officials, the provisions pertaining to reuse in both the department's original regulations and the amendment are intended to prevent collectors from stripping valuable components from used electronics for export to markets with poor environmental standards, and sending only the scrap with no value to the recyclers used by a standard or independent plan.

Similarly, a Washington refurbisher told us that the requirement for a part-for-part exchange when repairing equipment is intended to address the concern that collectors might export valuable components pulled out of equipment and receive a higher rate of compensation than by submitting the equipment to a recycler.

According to the refurbisher, the amendment has improved the impact of Washington's law on the ability to refurbish and reuse equipment but has also resulted in unnecessary work to reinstall components into equipment sent for recycling.

End Notes

[1] We use the term "recycling" in this report to refer to the full range of activities to reclaim components or usable materials from used electronic products. This term can be distinguished from the reuse or refurbishment of used electronics, which essentially results in the use of a product as originally intended, following any needed repair.

[2] EPA has developed regulations under the Resource Conservation and Recovery Act, as amended, to control hazardous waste from the time that it is generated until its ultimate disposal. 42 U.S.C. § 6901 et seq. (2010); 40 C.F.R. Pt. 260 et seq. (2010).

[3] GAO, Electronic Waste: EPA Needs to Better Control Harmful U.S. Exports through Stronger Enforcement and More Comprehensive Regulation, GAO-08-1044 (Washington, D.C.: Aug. 28, 2008).

[4] GAO, Electronic Waste: Strengthening the Role of the Federal Government in Encouraging Recycling and Reuse, GAO-06-47 (Washington, D.C.: Nov. 10, 2005).

[5] In this report, we do not include information on state electronics recycling legislation that, like legislation enacted by New York, establishes collection programs specifically for wireless telephones. Several stakeholders told us that recycling programs for wireless devices tend to differ from those for other electronics (e.g., because the small size of wireless devices facilitates mail-back programs).

[6] As of May 2010, EPA reported 108 one-time notifications for reuse. As of March 2010, EPA reported 16 notifications, with acknowledgments of consent from the receiving country, for a company to export CRTs for recycling. These documents are to specify the total quantity of CRTs, the destination recycling facility, and the specific time period of up to 12 months during which the exports may occur. All 16 consents to export came from two importing countries—Canada and the Republic of Korea.

[7] GAO-08-1044.

[8] Broken CRTs cannot be reused and, thus, may be exported only under the procedures applicable to CRTs exported for recycling—namely, the notice-and-consent requirement

[9] Any electronic products that meet the criteria for solid waste, such as when being recycled or disposed, and that also exhibit a hazardous characteristic, such as the toxicity characteristic for lead, are considered hazardous waste and fall within the regulations. To date, however,

EPA has promulgated specific regulations only for CRTs, as electronic products, and has indicated in Federal Register notices that other electronics generally do not possess hazardous characteristics under the regulatory rubric.

[10] Similarly, circuit boards, which are found in many electronic devices and contain mercury and other toxic substances, are subject to a special exemption from federal hazardous waste rules. This exemption is designed to ensure that circuit boards are treated as a valuable commodity, rather than as a waste. Circuit boards that meet the requirements of the exemption are not subject to any regulatory requirements when exported for recycling.

[11] According to EPA officials, the quantity of used electronics reported as collected for recycling by Plug-In To eCycling partners does not include the recycling that partners are responsible for or required to fund under state electronics recycling legislation.

[12] The Federal Electronics Challenge goals currently refer to the R2 practices as defining environmentally sound management.

[13] GAO, Federal Electronics Management: Federal Agencies Could Improve Participation in EPA's Initiatives for Environmentally Preferable Electronic Products, GAO-10-196T (Washington, D.C.: Oct. 27, 2009).

[14] To implement Executive Order 13423 requirements that address the purchase, operation and maintenance, and end-of-life management of electronic equipment, the Office of Management and Budget directed each agency and its facilities either to become a partner in the Federal Electronics Challenge or to implement an equivalent electronics stewardship program that is consistent with the Federal Electronics Challenge's recommended practices and guidelines.

[15] National Center for Electronics Recycling, A Study of the State-by-State E-Waste Patchwork: An analysis of its economic and other effects on industry, government and consumers (October 2006). One of the authors of the 2006 report told us that the document overestimated some costs (e.g., because the estimates are partially based on the cost of California implementing a recycling fee paid by consumers, which no other state has adopted) but underestimated other costs (e.g., costs for manufacturer participation in state study committees of options for electronics recycling legislation). As a result, he said that the report provides an accurate estimate of the inefficiencies associated with the state-by-state approach. We did not assess the reliability of the report's estimates.

[16] We did not attempt to compare collection and recycling rates among the five states because, in addition to states not having collection data prior to implementation of the recycling programs, each state's recycling legislation covers a different set of electronic devices as well as entities, such as households and small businesses, whose used electronics are covered. As a result, comparisons of collection rates would not provide a clear indication of the impact of various models of electronics recycling legislation.

[17] See N.H. Rev. Stat. Ann. § 149-M:27 (2010).

[18] The clearinghouse is modeled on a similar organization that focuses on toxics in packaging and works to reduce costs for state governments and the regulated community, in addition to providing consistency to the impacted industry.

[19] The National Center for Electronics Recycling is a nonprofit organization dedicated to the development and enhancement of a national infrastructure for the recycling of used electronics.

[20] GAO, Regulatory Programs: Balancing Federal and State Responsibilities for Standard Setting and Implementation, GAO-02-495 (Washington, D.C.: Mar. 20, 2002).

[21] GAO-08-1044.

End Notes for Appendix I

[1] GAO, Electronic Waste: EPA Needs to Better Control Harmful U.S. Exports through Stronger Enforcement and More Comprehensive Regulation, GAO-08-1044 (Washington, D.C.: Aug. 28, 2008).

End Notes for Appendix II

[1] As we have previously noted, for the purposes of this report, we consider recycling as distinct from reuse and refurbishment. In this appendix, however, we intend "recycling" to have the meaning given under the relevant state law. We also note any key ways in which a state program incorporates reuse or refurbishment.

[2] See California Electronic Waste Recycling Act of 2003, 2003 Cal. Legis. Serv. Ch. 526 (S.B. 20) (West), as amended by 2004 Cal. Legis. Serv. Ch. 863 (S.B. 50) (West), codified at Cal. Health & Safety Code §§ 21214.9-10.2 (2010), Cal. Pub. Res. Code §§ 41516, 42460-86 (2010) and others; Cal. Code Regs. tit. 14, §§ 18660.5–18660.43 (2010).

[3] See Me. Rev. Stat. Ann. Tit. 38, § 1610 (2010).

[4] Manufacturers also have the option of taking their own brands from the consolidator and sending the material to their preferred recycler.

[5] See Minn. Stat. §§ 115A.1310–1330 (2010).

[6] See 415 Ill. Comp. Stat. Ann. 150/1-999 (West 2010).

[7] See 2009-2010 Wisc. Legis. Serv. Act 50 (2009 S.B. 107) (West).

[8] See Tex. Health & Safety Code Ann. § 361.951–966 (Vernon 2010); 30 Tex. Admin. Code §§ 328.131-155 (2010).

[9] See Wash. Rev. Code §§ 70.95N.010-902 (2010).

In: Electronic Waste
Editors: J. L. Price and R. C. Cooper
ISBN 978-1-62081-617-2

Chapter 2

MANAGING ELECTRONIC WASTE: ISSUES WITH EXPORTING E-WASTE*

Linda Luther

SUMMARY

Electronic waste (e-waste) is a term that is used loosely to refer to obsolete, broken, or irreparable electronic devices like televisions, computer central processing units (CPUs), computer monitors (flat screen and cathode ray tubes), laptops, printers, scanners, and associated wiring. E-waste has become a concern in the United States due to the high volumes in which it is generated, the hazardous constituents it often contains (such as lead, mercury, and chromium), and the lack of regulations applicable to its disposal or recycling.

Under most circumstances, e-waste can legally be disposed of in a municipal solid waste landfill or recycled with few environmental regulatory requirements. Concerns about e-waste landfill disposal have led federal and state environmental agencies to encourage recycling. To date, 23 states have enacted some form of mandatory e-waste recycling program. These state requirements, mixed with increased consumer awareness regarding potential problems with landfilling e-waste, have led to an increase in recycling. With that increase have come new questions about e-waste management. Instead of questions only about the potential

* This is an edited, reformatted and augmented version of a Congressional Research Service publication, CRS Report for Congress R40850, from www.crs.gov, prepared for Members and Committees of Congress, dated September 27, 2010.

impacts associated with e-waste *disposal*, questions have arisen regarding the potential danger associated with e-waste *recycling*—particularly when recycling involves the export of e-waste to developing countries where there are few requirements to protect workers or the environment.

Answering questions about both e-waste disposal and recycling involves a host of challenges. For example, little information is available to allow a complete assessment of how e-waste is ultimately managed. General estimates have been made about the management of cathode ray tubes (CRTs, the only devices where disposal is federally regulated), but little reliable information is available regarding other categories of e-waste. For example, accurate data regarding how much is generated, how it is managed (through disposal or recycling), and where it is processed (domestically or abroad) are largely unknown. Further, little information is available regarding the total amount of functioning electronics exported to developing countries for legitimate reuse.

What *is* known is that e-waste recycling involves complex processes and it is more costly to recycle e-waste in the United States. It also is known that most consumer electronics manufacturers (who provide the market for material recovery from recycled electronics) have moved overseas. As a result, the majority of e-waste collected for recycling (either for reuse or recycling) appears to be exported for processing.

Although there may be limited data regarding how e-waste is managed, the consequences of export to developing countries that manage it improperly are becoming increasingly evident. In particular, various reports and studies (by the mainstream media, environmental organizations, and university researchers) have found primitive waste management practices in India and various countries in Africa and Asia. Operations in Guiyu in the Shantou region of China have gained particular attention. Observed recycling operations involve burning the plastic coverings of materials to extract metals for scrap, openly burning circuit boards to remove solder or soaking them in acid baths to strip them for gold or other metals. Acid baths are then dumped into surface water. Among other impacts to those areas have been elevated blood lead levels in children and soil and water contaminated with heavy metals.

The impacts associated with e-waste exports have led to concerns from environmental organizations, members of the public, and some Members of Congress.

INTRODUCTION

Electronic waste (e-waste) is a term that is used loosely to refer to obsolete, broken, or irreparable electronic devices like televisions, computer central processing units (CPUs), computer monitors (flat screen and cathode ray tubes), laptops, printers, scanners, and associated wiring. Rapid technology changes have led to increasingly large e-waste surpluses. Electronic devices, particularly older units in use today or in storage, contain a host of hazardous constituents such as lead, mercury, or chromium, as well as plastics treated with brominated flame retardants. The presence of these constituents has led to end-of-life (EOL) management[1] concerns from state and federal environmental agencies, environmental organizations, and some Members of Congress.

E-waste is essentially unregulated at the federal level—meaning it can be disposed of with common household garbage in municipal solid waste landfills (the primary disposal method) or incinerators. The Environmental Protection Agency (EPA) has stated that landfill disposal of e-waste is safe.[2] However, EPA's preferred method of EOL management is reuse or recycling. Further, state and local waste management agencies have expressed concerns regarding the potential cumulative impact to human health and the environment of landfilling millions of pounds of e-waste. As a result, individual states have begun to enact their own e-waste management requirements. To date, 23 states and New York City have enacted some form of e-waste management law. Those laws include provisions such as restrictions on landfill disposal of certain e-wastes and the establishment of mandatory recycling programs, generally paid for by electronics manufacturers. In the coming years, it is likely that more states will enact similar laws.

New state requirements, mixed with increased consumer awareness regarding potential problems with landfilling e-waste, have led to an increase in recycling. With that increase have come new questions about e-waste EOL management. Instead of questions only about the potential impacts associated with e-waste *disposal*, questions have arisen regarding the potential danger associated with e-waste *recycling*.

Because e-waste recycling is largely unregulated, virtually no data are available to track its fate.[3] Accurate data regarding how much is generated, how it is managed, and where it is processed (either domestically or abroad) are largely unavailable. What is known is that e-waste recycling may involve costly, complex processes and that there is an insufficient, though growing, national recycling infrastructure[4] to enable the United States to fully manage its own e-waste. It also is known that markets for e-waste (either for reuse or recycling for scrap) are largely overseas. As a result, the majority of e-waste collected for recycling appears to be exported for processing.

Although it is difficult to know exactly how much e-waste collected for recycling is exported, it appears that India or developing countries in Asia or Africa are most likely to receive it. Those countries are more likely to have electronics manufacturing plants that can cheaply repair or refurbish e-waste for reuse. Also, developing countries are more likely to value e-waste more highly than developed countries for its potential to recycle for scrap.

While some exports may be sent to facilities that manage e-waste in a way that protects workers and the environment, a significant amount is likely sent to countries that have few if any protections for workers or the environment, or that have regulations that are not enforced. The result is that recycling operations in those countries may pose a significant risk to human health and the environment. Increasingly, environmental organizations, university researchers, and the media have documented contamination to air, soil, and water, and health impacts to the people working and living near these operations—particularly to children (these issues are discussed in more detail in the section "Impacts of E-Waste Exports").

Concerns regarding the potential impact of exporting e-waste for processing in developing countries have led to increased scrutiny from members of the public and environmental organizations, as well as some Members of Congress. On May 21, 2009, Representative Gene Green introduced H.R. 2595, a bill that would amend the Solid Waste Disposal Act (42 U.S.C. 6921) to establish certain e-waste export restrictions. There have also been several congressional hearings on issues associated with e-waste management, one of which specifically addressed issues associated with e-waste exports.[5] There are various issues of concern with regard to e-waste disposal and recycling. This report looks at issues specifically related to its export for recycling. Particularly, it discusses documented impacts to human health and the environment that have been tied to unsafe recycling practices in developing countries.[6] It provides an overview of various factors necessary to understand why e-waste disposal has become a concern in the United States. Specifically, the report discusses issues that have motivated certain stakeholders to divert e-waste from landfill disposal and, hence, increase recycling. It also discusses waste management requirements in the United States, to illustrate how e-waste disposal and recycling are essentially unregulated; and why processing e-waste in undeveloped countries has, and will likely continue to have, a predominant role in the recycling process.

IMPACTS OF E-WASTE EXPORTS

It is difficult to determine how much e-waste is exported from the United States to developing countries. It is further difficult to determine how much of the waste that *is* exported is sent to facilities that will manage it safely as opposed to those that use disassembly and disposal methods that will expose workers to toxic chemicals with little, if any, protection. It is also difficult to determine how much e-waste may be sent to countries that have a limited regulatory framework to protect the local environment—potentially exposing the surrounding communities to resulting contamination.

What is becoming easier to document is the impact that e-waste exports are having on less developed nations. With increased exports have come increased media attention on the improper handling of e-waste in those areas and its resulting impacts.[7] Various reports have graphically documented health and safety threats to workers and environmental contamination from e-waste recovery practices in developing countries. It is difficult to document all e-waste recycling hubs, but popular destinations for e-waste exported from the United States (and other developed countries) are waste processing operations in Guiyu in the Shantou region of China, Delhi and Bangalore in India, and the Agbogbloshie site near Accra, Ghana.

Multiple studies have documented environmental and health effects of uncontrolled waste processing activities. Environmental impacts include contamination of all local environmental media—soil, air, surface water, and ground water. For example, a June 2009 study[8] found that the primary hazardous recycling operations in Guiyu involve

- metal recovery that involves open burning of wires to obtain steel and copper, cathode ray tube (CRT) cracking to obtain copper-laden yokes, desoldering and burning of circuit boards to remove solder and chips, and acid stripping chips for gold;
- plastic recycling through chipping and melting; and
- dumping of materials that cannot be further processed (such as leaded CRT glass and burned circuit boards) and residues from recycling operations (such as ashes from open burn operations, spent acid baths, and sludges).

It was observed that burning circuit board plastics treated with brominated flame retardants emitted harmful heavy metals, dioxins, and aromatic hydrocarbons. Further, heavy metal contamination in surface water and sediments was found that could be attributed to the direct effects of e-waste recycling operations in Guiyu. Copper from surface water was found to be 2.4 to 131 times the reference background concentrations, and sediment samples were 3.2 to 429 times the reference levels. The study also found severe levels of contamination for lead, cadmium, mercury, and arsenic in sediment and surface water as a result of recycling operations.

In addition to environmental contamination, impacts on humans have been observed. In a 2007 study, children from one to six years old in Guiyu were compared to those living in a neighboring town where no e waste processing was done.[9] Children in Guiyu were found to have blood lead levels (BLL) that were significantly higher than those in the neighboring village. The study concluded that elevated BLLs in Guiyu children were common as a result of exposure to lead contamination caused by primitive e-waste recycling activities.

CONCERNS ABOUT DOMESTIC E-WASTE DISPOSAL

To understand why e-waste is exported, it is helpful to understand why landfill disposal has become a concern to certain stakeholders in the United States. Those concerns center largely around the waste's increasing volume and the hazardous constituents, such as lead and mercury, it likely contains (particularly in older electronic devices). Increased awareness has encouraged state waste management and water resources agencies to consider the potential impacts to human health and the environment associated with e-waste and has led to increased efforts to divert e-waste from landfill disposal.

Waste Volume

The proliferation of and increasingly rapid technological advances in electronics mean that the volume of e-waste generated in the United States is large and growing. Data regarding electronic products sold, stored, recycled, and disposed of are limited. However, in 2008, EPA completed a study that attempted to gather more current data.[10] According to that study, in 2007, of the 2.25 million tons of televisions, cell phones and computer products ready for end-of-life (EOL) management, 18% (414,000 tons) were collected for recycling and 82% (1.84 million tons) were disposed of, primarily in landfills. Further, EPA estimated that approximately 235 million units sold between 1980 and 2007 were obsolete and in storage, awaiting some method of EOL management.

Although EPA estimates that e-waste comprises about 2% of the municipal solid waste stream, it is anticipated that this percentage will grow as consumers continue to replace old and outdated electronic equipment and discard equipment in storage.

Hazardous Constituents

Electronic devices may contain any of a host of hazardous constituents. Cathode ray tubes (CRTs)[11] found in televisions and computer monitors and printed circuit boards (PCBs, also referred to as printed wire boards, or PWBs), often contain significant amounts of lead.[12] CRTs contain an average of four pounds of lead but may contain more, depending on the size, age, and make of the device.

Although high lead levels in CRTs and PWBs often get the most attention from federal and state waste regulators, electronic devices such as personal and laptop computers, keyboards, and computer mice may contain toxic constituents such as arsenic, cadmium, chromium, or mercury.[13] In addition to potentially toxic constituents, plastics used in electronic devices often contain brominated flame retardants (BFRs). BFRs are widely used in plastic cases and cables for fire retardancy.[14] Plastics containing BFRs cannot be recycled as easily as plastics such as those used in plastic bottles or other containers.

While an individual electronic device may not have dangerously high levels of a given toxic material, the cumulative impact of large volumes of e-waste being disposed of in a municipal solid waste landfill has become troubling to many state waste management agencies.

E-Waste Management Requirements

Broadly speaking, discarded e-waste has two potential fates—it may be disposed of (most likely in a landfill) or it may be recycled. Once the device is in the hands of the recycler, it may be resold and reused "as is" or it may undergo some degree of refurbishing. Products that cannot be reused or refurbished are either dismantled or shredded, with the resulting material separated into secondary material streams and at least partially recovered. The resale of electronic devices for reuse or material recovery may occur domestically or abroad.

Regardless of whether an electronic device is disposed of or recycled, there are virtually no federal environmental regulatory requirements applicable to its management. Factors specific to e-waste that affect the lack of regulation are useful in understanding the challenges associated with addressing e-waste management issues.

Relevant Waste Disposal Requirements

Federal standards regarding waste management are specified under provisions of the Resource Conservation and Recovery Act (RCRA, 42 U.S.C. §6901 et seq.).[15] RCRA establishes criteria for managing both "solid" and "hazardous" waste. All regulatory requirements arising from the act stem from the initial determination of whether an item is actually a "waste" and, further, if that waste is "hazardous."

Solid waste is defined under the law as "any garbage, refuse ... or other discarded material." Subtitle D of RCRA establishes state and local governments as the primary planning, regulating, and implementing entities for the management of nonhazardous solid waste, such as household garbage and nonhazardous industrial solid waste. Landfills that collect household garbage are predominately regulated by state and local governments. EPA has, however, established minimum criteria that certain types of landfills must meet in order to stay open.[16]

Also under Subtitle D, states are encouraged (but not required by regulation) to develop comprehensive plans to manage nonhazardous industrial solid waste and municipal solid waste.

Under Subtitle C of RCRA, EPA has established regulations on the transport, treatment, storage, and disposal of "hazardous wastes." For a material to meet the regulatory definition of hazardous waste, it must first meet the definition of "solid waste." Further, for waste to be considered hazardous, it must either be listed specifically or exhibit any of four hazardous characteristics: ignitability, corrosivity, reactivity, and toxicity. E-waste would most likely exhibit toxicity characteristics, meaning it would be harmful or fatal when ingested or absorbed (because it contains toxic substances such as mercury or lead). When toxic wastes are disposed of on land, contaminated liquid may drain (leach) from the waste and pollute ground water. A common test method to determine the toxicity level of a waste is the Toxicity Characteristic Leaching Procedure (TCLP). The TCLP test is intended to simulate conditions that would likely occur in a landfill, and measures the potential for toxic constituents to seep or "leach" into groundwater.[17]

EPA has determined that CRTs and printed circuit boards meet the regulatory definition of hazardous waste, but has not determined if other electronic devices and components would consistently fail TCLP (i.e., exceed toxicity limits).

Studies have determined that devices such as personal computer central processing units (CPUs), laptop computers, printers, computer mice, and keyboards *have the potential to* exceed toxicity limits, but it has not been determined that entire classes of electronic devices will always be toxic.[18] Toxicity levels would likely vary by manufacturer, make, and model.

Even if a device meets the definition of hazardous waste, that does not necessarily mean that the device must be disposed of in accordance with RCRA's hazardous waste regulations.

EPA regulations have established many exclusions and exemptions to its hazardous waste disposal requirements.[19] Implementing exclusions or exemptions is often used as a mechanism to facilitate recycling. Examples of e-wastes that are excluded or exempt from the definition of hazardous waste are:

- Any electronic devices discarded by household consumers.
- Devices that can be reused.
- Scrap metal, processed scrap metal, precious metals, whole circuit boards, shredded circuit boards, processed CRT glass, intact CRTs, and partially processed CRTs sent for recycling.[20]

RCRA establishes certain minimum waste management standards that states must meet, but states have the option to implement requirements that are more stringent than those specified under RCRA.

To date, 23 states and New York City have opted to regulate e-waste more strictly. Although the specific requirements vary somewhat from state to state, all have the same goal—to avoid landfill disposal and incineration of certain types of e-waste.

Most state laws have certain broad elements in common, such as specifying the electronic devices covered under the law; how a collection and recycling program will be financed; collection and recycling criteria that must be met to minimize the impact to human health and the environment; and restrictions or requirements that products must meet to be sold in the state.

EPA's stated policy on e-waste management is to encourage equipment reuse, recycling, and then disposal, in that order.

Further, EPA has acknowledged that e-waste can be safely disposed of in municipal solid waste landfills. However, that is not its preferred management option.[21]

Recycling and Export Requirements

There are no federal laws that require e-waste recycling by commercial entities or households. Also, as with e-waste disposal, there are few federal environmental regulatory requirements applicable to recycling operations themselves (including the export of e-waste for recycling or reuse).

The term "recycler" broadly refers to a company that may engage in any of a number of activities including collecting, sorting, demanufacturing, or processing of waste. E-waste recycling can be a labor-intensive process (see "Factors Influencing E-Waste Exporting," below). Any federal regulation applicable to recycling operations would likely address human impacts associated with the disassembly process and apply to workplace health and safety operations. Any environmental regulations applicable to a recycling operation would likely apply to the management of residual waste generated during the recycling process.

Exporting e-waste is generally considered a potential element of the recycling process, wherein electronic devices are sent for reuse, refurbishment, or materials recovery. As with disposal and other elements of the recycling process, there are no requirements applicable to e-waste exporting as a whole. However, there are export notification requirements that apply to certain CRTs. Those requirements are stipulated under EPA's 2007 "CRT Rule."[22] Export notification requirements under the CRT Rule are summarized in *Table 1*, below.

High demand for used electronic products can facilitate illegal export—at least with respect to CRTs. Export notification requirements do not apply to CRTs exported for reuse. A recycler can export CRTs without notification by claiming such a purpose. In 2008, the Government Accountability Office (GAO) determined that EPA was not sufficiently enforcing the export notification requirements specified under the CRT Rule.[23] Since then, EPA has initiated enforcement actions against several recyclers for not submitting the proper notifications.

In addition to a lack of regulatory restrictions on recycling activities, there are currently no consistently applied industry standards applicable to e-waste recyclers. This can actually pose a problem to recyclers that limit their exports.

A recycler that removes hazardous constituents from e-waste, sorts and disassembles its e-waste, and exports the waste to a responsible recycler or confirms that devices are in working order before exporting them for reuse, will likely offer its services at a significantly higher rate than a recycler that simply ships unsorted e-waste abroad. The recycler that ships unsorted e-waste can still make the claim that it is operating in a "green" way because it diverts the waste from landfill disposal. A recycler can also claim that it does not export its waste, but that is a claim that would be very hard for the average consumer (or even a state or charitable organization using the recycler) to confirm.

Table 1. Summary of the CRT Rule's Export Notification Requirements

Type of CRT Subject to Regulation	Overview of Regulatory Requirements
Used CRTs (Broken and Intact) Exported for Recycling	Used CRTs exported for recycling must comply with requirements specified in 40 CFR 261.39(a)(5), including requirements to notify EPA of an intended shipment 60 days before the shipment. Notification may cover exports extending over a 12-month or shorter period and must include contact information about the exporter and recycler, and an alternate recycler. It must also include a description of the recycling, frequency and rate of export, means of transport, total quantity of CRTs, and information about transit countries. Consent is not required from transit countries, but EPA will notify the exporter of any responses from these countries.
CRT Glass Exported for Recycling	Processed glass (i.e., CRT glass that has been removed from the monitor and sorted from other material) is not subject to export requirements. Unsorted glass would be considered a "broken CRT" and would be subject to export requirements.
Used Intact CRTs Exported for Reuse	Persons who export used, intact CRTs for reuse must submit a one-time notification to the appropriate EPA Region with contact information and a statement that they are exporting the CRTs for reuse.
Unused Intact CRTs Exported for Reuse or Recycling	No regulatory requirements

Source: Table generated by the Congressional Research Service (CRS) using information from the Environmental Protection Agency's Web page, "Final Rules on Cathode Ray Tubes and Discarded Mercury-Containing Equipment," available online at http://www.epa.gov/osw/hazard/recycling/electron/index.htm.

Voluntary Efforts

Various electronics manufacturers have adopted company polices that address issues associated with exports to developing countries. For example, Hewlett-Packard (HP) and Dell have adopted company policies that ban exports of nonworking electronics to developing countries.

Also, since 2008, voluntary recycler certification programs have been developed by environmental organizations, the recycling industry, and EPA. Certification programs implemented by environmental organizations, such as the Basel Action Network's "E-Stewards" program, would prohibit certain e-waste exports.[24] EPA's "Responsible Recycling (R2) Practices" program specifies that a recycler exporting e-waste must obtain "assurances from downstream vendors both domestically and internationally ... [that] show that the materials are being handled properly and legally by downstream vendors throughout the recycling chain."[25]

Any impact these voluntary certification programs may have has yet to be seen. At this point, it is difficult to determine how effectively voluntary certification programs may be enforced. It is also difficult to determine if voluntary programs will have an effect on companies willing to make false or misleading claims about the environmental attributes of their recycling services.

FACTORS INFLUENCING E-WASTE EXPORTING

Since e-waste recycling is largely unregulated, accurate data regarding the end markets, both domestic and abroad, are not publicly available. Therefore, it is difficult to know how much e-waste that is collected for recycling is actually exported for processing. However, in a 2008 report, EPA consulted an industry expert to develop a "best estimate" of the end markets for CRT-containing devices (televisions and computer monitors). According to that estimate, between 77% and 89% of those end markets were outside the United States.26 EPA acknowledged that such data are fluid—market conditions change rapidly. Also, since this estimate only applies only to CRTs, it is not possible to apply those estimates to all e-waste. Still, it can be estimated that the majority of e-waste collected for recycling is processed, at least to some extent, abroad.

There are various reasons why recyclers export e-waste instead of recycling it domestically. Most reasons relate to the high costs of processing the waste domestically and the lower costs and higher demand for the material abroad.

Costly and Complex Domestic Recycling Processes

E-waste collected for recycling may be reused or processed for parts or components. Before it can be determined which of those two fates it may meet, the device will require a certain level of sorting, inspection, and testing.

If a product is ultimately processed for parts or components, it would have to go through various processing activities. Unlike recyclable products that contain essentially a single component, like plastic bottles or newspaper, electronic devices contain a host of mixed materials that may not be easily separated or extracted.

Before the device can be recycled it may go through any of a number of steps, including some or all of the following:[27]

- *Demanufacturing into subassemblies and components*—involves a worker manually disassembling a device or component to recover value from working and nonworking components (e.g., video cards, circuit boards, cables, wiring, plastic or metal housing).
- *Depollution*—the removal and separation of certain materials to allow them to be handled separately to minimize impacts to human health and the environment (e.g., batteries, fluorescent lamps, CRTs, or plastics embedded with brominated flame retardants).
- *Materials separation*—manually separating and preparing material for further processing. At this stage, materials that have already been disassembled would be sorted into material categories.
- *Mechanical processing of similar materials*—generally involves processing compatible plastic resins, metals, or CRT glass to generate market-grade commodities.
- *Mechanical processing of mixed materials*—generally involves processing whole units, after depollution, followed by a series of separation technologies.
- *Metal refining/smelting*—after being sorted into components or into shredded streams, metals can be sent to refiners or smelters. At this stage, thermal and chemical management processes are used to extract metals of many types.

Many of the processes described above must be done by hand and can be labor intensive. This can be a costly operation. Depending on the value of the commodities being extracted, among other factors, a recycler may find it more profitable simply to send all of the e-waste it collects abroad, where labor is less costly but health and safety practices may not be implemented when extracting hazardous materials or precious metals. If an e-waste collector or recycler offers its services for free, it likely ships whole units abroad.

Limited Domestic Recycling

Limits on domestic recycling apply to both the infrastructure (the network of waste collection, transportation, and sorting activities) and the actual processing of the waste. Compared to paper, glass, and plastic recycling, electronic recycling has a short history. An e-waste recycling infrastructure is still being developed.

E-waste may be collected at state- or locally-sponsored household hazardous waste collection sites or events (meaning, it is not collected on an on-going basis, but may be collected semimonthly or semi-annually). E-waste may also be collected at manufacturer or retailer sponsored events. Regardless of where it is collected or who is responsible for collecting it—consumers will likely be required to drop off their e-waste.

According to the Government Accountability Office (GAO), cost and inconvenience inhibit consumers from recycling used electronics.[28] Most stakeholders agree that if e-waste is to be recycled, it must be as easy for consumers to recycle electronics as it is to buy them. Many local and state agencies, retailers, and electronics manufacturers have worked with EPA to sponsor pilot programs providing convenient, free recycling services to consumers. [29] Although such events often collect large amounts of e-waste, it is difficult to determine what happens to the waste after collection.

The extent to which e-waste may be processed domestically after collection is also limited. A company that operates as a "recycler" may actually be a waste consolidator that sends the waste to another vendor to sort or process it in some way. Those downstream vendors may separate the units for reuse, ship whole units abroad for processing, or process it domestically to some degree (see the list of potential steps in recycling under "Costly and Complex Domestic Recycling Processes," above).

However, once a unit has been broken down into its component parts, the presence of recycling facilities with the ability and capacity to recycle those components is limited, and varies from region to region. For example, there are few facilities in the United States capable of processing CRT glass. There are also limited opportunities in the United States for copper and precious metal recovery from circuit boards or for processing flame retardant-containing plastic.

Further, most consumer electronics manufacturers (who provide the market for materials recovered from recycled electronics) have manufacturing operations overseas.

For example, almost all glass manufacturers that may reuse CRT glass are located overseas.

High Demand Abroad

Demand abroad is high in both recycling and reuse markets. When U.S. consumers discard electronic products, they are not necessarily broken. In developing countries, there is high demand for electronics that American consumers may deem "waste."

According to EPA estimates, in 2005, 61% of CRTs collected for recycling were refurbished or remanufactured into new televisions abroad.[30] Also, a study specific to exports to Peru found that 85% of used personal computers (PCs) imported by Peru were reused rather than recycled. [31] The study concluded that decisions regarding the end-of-life management of computers were driven by reuse as opposed to recycling.[32]

Further, in 2008, GAO reported that there is significant demand for used electronics in developing countries. In particular, GAO reported:

> In a search of one Internet e-commerce site, we observed brokers from around the world place 2,234 requests to purchase liquid-crystal display (LCD) screens.
>
> On the same site, we found 430 requests for central processing units and 665 requests for used computers. In an extensive search of two Internet e-commerce sites over a 3-month period, we observed brokers in developing countries make 230 requests for about 7.5 million used CRTs. Brokers in developing countries represented over 60 percent of all requests we observed.33

Developing countries also have a high demand for scrap. Demand for plastics for recycling is almost entirely overseas.

CONCLUSION

An unintended consequence of avoiding *potential* negative impacts of domestic e-waste disposal has been a contribution to *actual* environmental contamination and human health impacts to some communities in developing countries.

If environmentally preferable management of e-waste is the goal, is recycling it preferable to landfill disposal if recycling means exporting the waste to developing countries? Determining how to address this issue—that is, take into consideration concerns regarding domestic e-waste disposal *and* the negative impacts of recycling abroad— involves many factors.

One significant factor is the lack of timely, accurate data needed to help fully understand the scope of the potential problem. It is almost impossible to know exactly how much e-waste is generated, to what extent it is processed domestically (e.g., to what degree it is sorted or disassembled by domestic recyclers), how much is exported, and, of the waste that *is* exported, how much is actually reusable or sent to a facility that will manage it properly. That is not to say that all or even the majority of e-waste that is exported is managed improperly. It is simply impossible to know using existing data.

Electronics manufacturers are currently driven by various forces to make their products more easily recyclable and with fewer hazardous constituents.[34] Any *future* changes to electronic devices have no impact, however, on the hundreds of millions of devices currently in use or obsolete devices currently in storage.

Eventually those devices will make their way to the disposal or recycling markets.

The high cost of domestic recycling, high demand for exports, and a lack of barriers to export will continue to drive reuse and recycling markets abroad. As stated previously, the current regulatory structure involves no or very limited prohibition on exports and limited options for reuse or recycling (although, those options will likely increase as e-waste collection increases). As long as there are legitimate reuse markets and recycling operations in developing countries, an *outright* prohibition on exports would be problematic, particularly when limited opportunities for recycling exist in the United States. This presents policy-makers with multiple challenges: principal among them are how to address the obstacles that limit domestic recycling, and how one might establish export controls that facilitate reuse and recycling but prohibit delivery of e-waste to operations that do not protect workers or their environment.

End Notes

[1] EOL management options include disposal (in a landfill or through incineration) or recycling (which may include reprocessing for parts or refurbishment and reuse). While reuse may be considered a form of recycling, in this report, "recycling" will generally refer to recovering a device for the purposes of dismantling and parts or materials recovery. "Reuse" will include the reuse of a device "as is" or with refurbishment.

[2] For more information, see Robert Tonetti, EPA Office of Solid Waste, presentation materials, "EPA's Regulatory Program for E-Waste," October 2007, available online at http://www.epa.gov/waste/conserve/materials/ecycling/docs/ e-wasteregs.pdf.

[3] Most available waste management data attempt to approximate disposal, recycling, or export information about cathode ray tubes (CRTs). Little, if any, data are available regarding the generation, disposal, or recycling of other types of e-waste such as flat panel monitors, CPUs, or laptops.

[4] Although not defined in law or regulation, in this report, "recycling infrastructure" refers to collection, transportation, and processing of e-waste for reuse or recycling.

[5] House Committee on Foreign Affairs, Subcommittee on Asia, the Pacific and the Global Environment, "Exporting Toxic Trash: Are We Dumping Our Electronic Waste on Poorer Countries?" September 17, 2008. For more information, see http://www.international relations.house.gov/hearing_notice.asp?id=1031.

[6] The primary focus of this report is on issues associated with exports to developing countries. It does not look at exports and recycling operations in developed countries that may operate in a manner that protects both its workers and the environment.

[7] See FRONTLINE/World, "Ghana, Digital Dumping Ground," originally broadcast June 23, 2009, available online at http://www.pbs.org/frontlineworld/stories/ghana804/video/video_ index.html; 60 Minutes, "Following the Trail of Toxic E-Waste," broadcast November 9, 2008, and August 27, 2009, available online at http://www.cbsnews.com/ stories/2009/ 08/19/60minutes/main4579229.shtml; National Geographic, "High Tech Trash," January 2008, available online at http://ngm.nationalgeographic.com/2008/01/high-tech-trash/ carroll-text; Basel Action Network and Silicon Valley Toxics Coalition, "Exporting Harm: The High Tech Trashing of Asia," February 25, 2002, available online at http://www.ban.org/E-waste/technotrashfinalcomp.pdf; Scientific American, "Not in My Backyard: Stopping Illegal Export of Junked Televisions and Computers," November 19, 2008, available online at http://www.scientificamerican.com/article.cfm?id=stopping-illegal -e-waste-export-and-mishandling; BusinessWeek, "E-Waste: The Dirty Secret of Recycling Electronics," October 15, 2008, available online at http://www.businessweek. com/ magazine/content/08_43/b4105000160974.htm.

[8] Yan Guoa, et al., Journal of Environmental Quality, "Heavy Metals in the Environment: Heavy Metal Contamination from Electronic Waste Recycling at Guiyu, Southeastern China," July-August, 2009, Vol. 38:1617-1626.

[9] Xia Huo, et al., Environmental Health Perspectives, "Elevated Blood Lead Levels of Children in Guiyu, an Electronic Waste Recycling Town in China," Vol. 115, Number 7, July 2007, 1113-1117.

[10] EPA published the final results of its study on "Electronics Waste Management in the United States" in July 2008. The consumer electronics covered in EPA's analyses are televisions, personal computers (desktops, laptops, and computer monitors), hard copy computer peripherals (including printers, scanners, and fax machines), computer mice, keyboards, and cell phones. EPA used two different approaches to gather its data. Summary information

about the study as well as the results of each approach is available on EPA's Web page, "Statistics on the Management of Used and End-of-Life Electronics," at http://www.epa.gov/waste/conserve/materials/ecycling/manage.htm.

[11] CRTs are the large vacuum tubes that provide the video display in older televisions and computer monitors.

[12] Lead is a toxic metal that can cause delayed neurological development in children and other adverse health effects in adults, including increased blood pressure, nephritis, and cerebro-vascular disease. For more information, see EPA's Final Rule, "Hazardous Waste Management System; Modification of the Hazardous Waste Program; Cathode Ray Tubes," 71 Fed. Reg. 42927 July 28, 2006.

[13] See report prepared by Timothy G. Townsend, et al, "RCRA Toxicity Characterization of Computer CPUs and Other Electronic Devices," by Department of Environmental Engineering Sciences the University of Florida, Gainesville, Sponsored by EPA Regions 4 and 5, July 15, 2004.

[14] Polybrominated diphenyl ethers (PBDEs) are the most commonly used brominated flame retardants (BFRs) which became a replacement for polychlorinated biphenyls (PCBs). The extent to which PBDEs pose a threat to human health is unclear (see the Department of Health and Human Services, Agency for Toxic Substances and Disease Registry, ToxFAQsTM for PBDEs, available online at http://www.atsdr.cdc.gov/tfacts68-pbde.html). However, concerns about the potential impacts of the use of BFRs have led some countries to ban their use and some manufacturers to voluntarily phase-out their use. Also, some U.S. states have banned their use. (For more information, see the Organisation for Economic Co-Operation and Development Web page regarding "Brominated Flame Retardants," see particularly the Hazard/Risk Information Sheets, available online at http://www.oecd.org/document/63/ 0,3343,en_2649_34375_2403647_1_1_1_1,00.html.) However, BFRs are present in many devices still on the market, in use, or in storage.

[15] The Solid Waste Disposal Act (SWDA), enacted by Congress in 1965, provided federal statutory provisions regarding solid waste disposal practices. RCRA was a 1976 amendment to SWDA. All subsequent amendments to SWDA, including the Hazardous and Solid Waste Amendments (HSWA, P.L. 98-616) of 1984 and the Federal Facilities Compliance Act (FFCA, P.L. 102-386) of 1992, are commonly referred to as RCRA.

[16] For more information about landfill standards, see EPA's "Landfills" website at http://www.epa.gov/osw/nonhaz/ municipal/landfill.htm.

[17] TCLP is not the only approved method to determine a waste's toxicity. Other test methods may also be acceptable. For more information, see EPA's website regarding various test methods for evaluating solid waste, at http://www.epa.gov/waste/hazard/ testmethods /index.htm.

[18] See footnote 13, Timothy G. Townsend, et al, "RCRA Toxicity Characterization of Computer CPUs and Other Electronic Devices," p. 5-1.

[19] An "exclusion" is a situation where a designated material would be deemed a "non-waste" that is, it is excluded from the definition of solid waste and, therefore, could not be defined as a hazardous waste. An "exemption" is a situation where the material is considered a waste, but specifically exempted from the definition of hazardous waste.

[20] For more information see EPA's eCycling "Regulations/Standards" Web page, http://www.epa.gov/waste/conserve/ materials/ecycling/rules.htm. Regulatory exclusions specific to CRTs are specified in regulations that have come to be referred to as the "CRT Rule"; see EPA's Final Rule, "Hazardous Waste Management System; Modification of the Hazardous Waste Program; Cathode Ray Tubes," 71 Fed. Reg. 42927 July 28, 2006.

[21] Robert Tonetti, EPA Office of Solid Waste, presentation materials "EPA's Regulatory Program for E-Waste," October 2007, available online at http://www.epa.gov/waste/ con serve/materials/ecycling/docs/e-wasteregs.pdf.

[22] See footnote 20.

[23] Government Accountability Office report to the Chairman, Committee on Foreign Affairs, House of Representatives, "Electronic Waste: EPA Needs to Better Control Harmful U.S. Exports through Stronger Enforcement and More Comprehensive Regulation," report GAO 08-1044, August 2008, available online at http://www.gao.gov/new.items/ d081044.pdf.

[24] For information about the Basel Action Network's "E-Stewards Certification Program," go to http://www.estewards.org/esteward_certification.html.

[25] See EPA's "Responsible Recycling (R2) Practices" available online at http://www.epa.gov/ waste/conserve/materials/ ecycling/r2practices.htm.

[26] See the EPA's Office of Solid Waste, "Electronic Waste Management in the United States: Approach 1," EPA530-R08-009, July 2008, p. 29. Available online at http://www.epa.gov/ epawaste/conserve/materials/ecycling/manage.htm.

[27] Activities listed here are specified in "Closing the Loop: Electronics Design to Enhance Reuse/Recycling Value," a study conducted by the Green Electronics Council and funded through a cooperative agreement with EPA's Office of Solid Waste and Emergency Response Innovations Pilot Projects, pp. 5-7, January 2009. The report is available online at http://www.greenelectronicscouncil.org/documents/0000/0007/Design_for_End_of_Life_Fi nal_Report_090208.pdf.

[28] Statement of John B. Stephenson, Director, Government Accountability Office (GAO) Natural Resources and Environment, before the Subcommittee on Superfund and Waste Management, Committee on Environment and Public Works, U.S. Senate, "Electronic Waste: Observations on the Role of the Federal Government in Encouraging Recycling and Reuse," July 25, 2005, pp. 8-10.

[29] EPA lists information about e-waste recycling on its website at http://www.epa.gov/ epawaste/conserve/materials/ ecycling/donate.htm. Information provided is from not-for-profit organizations, industry associations, electronics manufacturers, and electronics retailers.

[30] See EPA's "Electronic Waste Management in the United States: Approach 1," pp. 31-32.

[31] Ramzy Kahhat, Eric Williams, "Product or Waste? Importation and End-of-Life Processing of Computers in Peru," Environmental Science & Technology, 2009 43 (15), 6010-6016.

[32] Still, the study found that when PCs were eventually disposed of, they may not be processed properly.

[33] See GAO's "Electronic Waste: EPA Needs to Better Control Harmful U.S. Exports through Stronger Enforcement and More Comprehensive Regulation," p. 16.

[34] These forces include consumer demand for "greener" products and regulatory restrictions on the use of hazardous substances. Regulatory restrictions are being developed primarily outside the United States. For example, European Union (EU) Directive 2002/95/EC is the restriction on the use of certain hazardous substances (RoHS) in electrical and electronic equipment. The RoHS Directive bans the use of certain heavy metals and brominated flame retardants from certain electronic equipment. Further, EU Directive 2002/96/EC on waste electrical and electronic equipment (WEEE) includes provisions that encourage the design and production of electronic equipment that will facilitate dismantling and recovery, particularly the reuse and recycling of electronic equipment.

In: Electronic Waste
Editors: J. L. Price and R. C. Cooper

ISBN 978-1-62081-617-2

Chapter 3

ISSUES IN INTERNATIONAL TRADE LAW: RESTRICTING EXPORTS OF ELECTRONIC WASTE*

Emily C. Barbour

SUMMARY

Electronic waste (e-waste) is a term that loosely refers to obsolete, broken, or irreparable electronic devices like televisions, computer central processing units (CPUs), computer monitors, laptops, printers, scanners, and associated wiring. Because e-waste is generated in high volumes in the United States and contains hazardous materials like lead, mercury, and chromium, it is a growing area of domestic concern. Currently, e-waste is essentially unregulated at the federal level and can be disposed of with common household garbage in municipal solid waste landfills or incinerators. However, the international trade in e-waste is subject to the international agreements governing the hazardous waste trade. The United States is a party to several of these agreements, but it is not a party to the largest multilateral agreement in this field: the Basel Convention.

Although it is difficult to know exactly how much e-waste is exported from the United States, developing countries in Asia or Africa appear to be active importers of it. Many of these countries lack, or do not

* This is an edited, reformatted and augmented version of a Congressional Research Service publication, CRS Report for Congress R42373, from www.crs.gov, prepared for Members and Committees of Congress, dated February 24, 2012.

enforce, labor or environmental laws that would mitigate or prevent the harms to human and environmental health that are associated with e-waste processing. The result is that some overseas e-waste recycling operations may pose a significant risk to human and environmental well-being.

Recently, momentum has developed for domestic legislation restricting U.S. e-waste exports. These restrictions could take many forms, including a partial or total ban on e-waste exports, an e-waste export licensing system, or a quota on e-waste exports. However, these restrictions may be difficult to reconcile with the General Agreement on Tariffs and Trade (GATT), one of the World Trade Organization (WTO) Agreements, and could be susceptible to challenge before a WTO panel.

In particular, e-waste export restrictions may be deemed inconsistent with Articles XI:1, XIII:1, and I:1 of the GATT. If declared a violation of the GATT, e-waste export restrictions could be justified under Article XX of the GATT if they (1) fit under one of the exceptions listed in paragraphs (a) to (j) of Article XX of the GATT and (2) satisfy the requirements imposed by the Article XX chapeau. It would be difficult, however, for U.S. export restrictions on e-waste to meet this standard for justification if they are imposed without serious U.S. engagement in international negotiations on the hazardous waste trade or without the concurrent operation of comparable restrictions on domestic e-waste production.

INTRODUCTION

Electronic waste (e-waste) is a term that refers loosely to obsolete, broken, or irreparable electronic devices like televisions, computer central processing units (CPUs), computer monitors (flat screen and cathode ray tubes), laptops, printers, scanners, and associated wiring. E-waste has become a concern in the United States in part because of the high volumes in which it is generated and the hazardous ingredients it often contains (such as lead, mercury, and chromium).

E-waste is essentially unregulated at the federal level—meaning it can be disposed of with common household garbage in municipal solid waste landfills (the primary disposal method) or incinerators.[1] U.S. producers of e-waste may also opt to export it overseas for processing. Although it is difficult to know exactly how much e-waste is exported, developing countries in Asia or Africa appear to be active importers of it. Many of these countries lack, or do not enforce, labor or environmental laws that would mitigate or prevent the harms associated with e-waste processing. The result is that e-waste recycling operations in those countries may pose a significant risk to human health and the environment. Environmental impacts reportedly include contamination of the local soil, air, surface water, and groundwater.

Although the United States has been involved in international efforts aimed at regulating the transboundary movements of hazardous waste for decades, it is not a party to the primary multilateral agreement governing the international waste trade: the Basel Convention on the Control of Transboundary Movements of Hazardous Wastes and Their Disposal (Basel Convention). This Convention forbids parties from exporting hazardous wastes to a party who has not received notice of, and consented to, that export. It also requires parties to adopt domestic policies aimed at reducing the production of hazardous waste. An amendment to that Convention, which has not yet entered into force, would ban hazardous waste exports from "Annex VII" parties—members of the OECD, European Union, and Liechtenstein—to other Convention parties, which are primarily developing countries.

Recently, momentum has developed for domestic legislation restricting e-waste exports from the United States. These restrictions could take many forms, including a ban akin to the one proposed by the Ban Amendment to the Basel Convention, an e-waste export licensing system, or a quota on e-waste exports.

These restrictions may be difficult to reconcile with the General Agreement on Tariffs and Trade (GATT), one of the World Trade Organization (WTO) Agreements, and could be susceptible to challenge before a WTO panel.

International Agreements on Hazardous Waste

Since the 1980s, the United States has been a party to international agreements governing the transboundary movements of hazardous wastes.[2] These agreements, one among the member countries of the Organization for Economic Cooperation and Development (OECD) and two bilateral agreements with Canada and Mexico, condition hazardous waste exports on the notification of both exporting and destination countries and the destination country's consent.[3] However, these agreements cover a broader category of waste—all hazardous waste—than the hazardous *electronic* waste commonly called e-waste.

Although the United States has engaged in some international efforts to regulate hazardous waste exports, it is not a party to the primary multilateral agreement governing the international waste trade: the Basel Convention on the Control of Transboundary Movements of Hazardous Wastes and Their Disposal (Basel Convention).[4] Over 170 other countries are parties to the Basel Convention, which was negotiated under the auspices of the United Nations Environment Programme.[5] The Basel Convention forbids parties from exporting hazardous wastes to any other party who has not received notice of, and consented to, that export. Article 4 of the Basel Convention imposes several other prohibitions and obligations on the parties, including, *inter alia*:

- a prohibition on the export of hazardous wastes to (or importing hazardous wastes from) non-parties unless the exporting and importing countries have entered into an international agreement with provisions on environmentally sound waste management that are at least equivalent to those in the Convention;
- an obligation to ensure that the generation of hazardous wastes within their territories is reduced to a minimum;
- a requirement to prohibit persons within their jurisdictions from transporting hazardous wastes unless they are authorized to do so; and
- an obligation to require that hazardous waste exports are managed in an environmentally sound manner in the state of import.

In addition, in 1995, Basel Convention parties adopted an amendment to the Convention to impose an absolute ban on hazardous waste export from "Annex VII" parties—members of the OECD, European Union, and Liechtenstein—to other Convention parties, which are primarily developing countries.[6] Although some parties implemented the ban domestically, the "Ban Amendment" has not entered into force.[7]

THE GENERAL AGREEMENT ON TARIFFS AND TRADE

The General Agreement on Tariffs and Trade (GATT) is one of the foundational agreements of the WTO's legal regime. At its most general, the GATT sets the maximum tariffs for particular goods and disciplines certain trade-restricting measures adopted by WTO Members.[8] Among the GATT's cornerstone provisions are Article XI, which prohibits quantitative prohibitions or restrictions on the exportation of goods to any other Member country, and Article I, which bans measures that grant less favorable treatment to the products of one WTO Member country than to the like products of any other country.

The WTO Understanding on Rules and Procedures Governing the Settlement of Disputes (DSU) provides a means for WTO Members to resolve disputes arising under WTO agreements.[9] WTO Members must first attempt to settle their dispute through consultations, but, if these fail, the Member initiating the dispute may request that a panel examine and report on its complaint. In addition, a Member may appeal a panel's report to the WTO Appellate Body. Members whose measures are deemed inconsistent with its WTO obligations and unjustified under one of the GATT exceptions, such as those in Article XX, are expected to implement the panel and/or Appellate Body's report. That is, the defending Member must withdraw, modify, or replace its inconsistent measures. If a disagreement arises as to whether the defending Member has, in fact, implemented the report, a WTO panel may be convened to hear the dispute over compliance. The WTO Appellate Body hears appeals of these compliance panel reports.

Ultimately, when a defending Member fails to implement a panel or Appellate Body report within the established compliance period, the prevailing Member may request that the defending Member negotiate a compensation agreement. If these negotiations are not requested or if an agreement is not reached, the prevailing Member may also request authorization to impose certain trade sanctions against the non-complying Member. Specifically, the WTO may authorize the prevailing Member to suspend tariff concessions or other trade obligations that it otherwise owes the non-complying Member under a WTO agreement.

Article XI

Article XI:1 of the GATT bars the institution or maintenance of quantitative restrictions on exports to, and imports from, any WTO Member's territory. Quantitative restrictions limit the amount of a product that may be imported or exported.

Common examples are embargoes, quotas, minimum import or export prices, and certain import or export licensing requirements. Only duties, taxes, and other charges are Article XI:1 consistent methods of restricting imports or exports.

Article XI:1's constraints apply to a broad range of government actions (all "measures")— including those, like government agency practices, that are not required by a law or regulation.[10] Article XI prohibits WTO Members from taking these actions if they impose or have the effect of a quantitative restriction.[11] Moreover, a measure that expressly institutes an import or export ban constitutes a quantitative restriction within the meaning of Article XI:1 regardless of whether it has, in practice, impeded imports or exports.[12] Because the GATT protects both existing and future trade flows, a measure that *would*, by its terms, preclude certain potential exports is inconsistent with Article XI:1.[13]

To date, only a few WTO panels have considered *export* restrictions under Article XI:1. However, measures that ban or impose a licensing system on e-waste exports could constitute export restrictions prohibited by Article XI:1.

Imposing a Ban on E-Waste Exports

As discussed above, any government action that expressly precludes the importation or exportation of certain goods constitutes a quantitative restriction *per se* and is necessarily inconsistent with the GATT. Although there are few GATT or WTO panel decisions on export bans, as discussed below, panels have consistently found that *import* bans implemented through compulsory licensing systems violate Article XI. This jurisprudence can be expected to inform any WTO panel decision on the GATT consistency of export bans and licensing.[14]

Brazil – Tyres[15] is one example of a WTO panel decision striking down an import ban implemented through a licensing system. In that case, the European Union challenged the GATT consistency of a set of Brazilian laws designed to limit imports of certain products—retreaded tires—that Brazil believed had a negative environmental impact. Specifically, Brazil had adopted a licensing system under which a person could only import retreaded tires after obtaining a license, but a person would be ineligible for this license when the retreaded tire imports originated in a non-MERCOSUR country.[16] Although the panel acknowledged that Brazil did not explicitly prohibit retreaded tire imports from non-MERCOSUR countries, it found that because no person could obtain the license required to import these goods, the licensing measure plainly "operate[d] so as to prohibit" their importation. The panel therefore held that the measure constituted an import ban barred by Article XI:1 of the GATT.[17]

In another dispute over a licensing system, *India – Quantitative Restrictions*,[18] a WTO panel struck down a measure under which both exporters sending specified goods to India and importers bringing specified goods into India were required to obtain a license. [19] The measure established license eligibility criteria that distinguished between importers on the basis of their reasons for importing the covered goods. An importer was ineligible for a license if it was importing the goods for resale, but an entity importing the goods for its own direct use *was* eligible for the compulsory license.[20] The panel found that a licensing system based on this distinction was inconsistent with Article XI:1 because it limited the amount of covered imports by precluding some entities from importing those goods at all.[21]

Imposing a Licensing System on E-Waste Exports

A government action that operates as "any form of limitation... on, or in relation to" imports or exports is prohibited by Article XI:1.[22] Whether a measure meets this standard is assessed by its design and "its potential to adversely affect" exportation.[23] WTO panels have consistently described "discretionary" or "non-automatic" licensing requirements as falling within this category of prohibited quantitative restrictions.[24] As a result, a system under which the licensing authority has universally granted licenses to applicants who satisfy the prerequisites may still violate Article XI:1 if those prerequisites give the licensing authority unfettered discretion to deny a license.[25]

The WTO panel decision in *China – Raw Materials*,[26] suggests that a measure could be inconsistent with Article XI:1 if it, or its implementing regulations, prescribe vague or unspecified criteria for granting licenses. In that case, a WTO panel assessed the GATT consistency of China's export licensing system for certain raw materials (bauxite, fluorspar, etc.) and rejected China's argument that the licensing system was "automatic" because no qualified applicant had been denied a license.[27] Instead, the panel found that some of the criteria for a license were worded so vaguely as to be "unspecified," which endowed the Chinese licensing authorities with unfettered discretion to deny a license.[28] The panel singled out one qualification in particular: the requirement that the license application be "complete and accurate." The panel wrote that rather than specifying *how* an application could meet this qualification, the law authorized the licensing agencies to require applicants to submit unspecified "documents of approval" and "other materials."[29] As a result, it was impossible, in the panel's view, for an applicant to know what documents would be necessary to qualify for a license.[30] This uncertainty would, the panel reasoned, discourage some exporters from seeking export licenses at all and, in doing so, cause an overall reduction in exports of raw materials.[31] The panel therefore ruled that, by giving its licensing authorities the flexibility to require documents not expressly enumerated in the law, China had created a discretionary licensing system that restrained exports of raw materials in violation of Article XI:1 of the GATT.[32] In the United States, presumably, principles of constitutional due process forbid an agency from basing e-waste export licensing decisions on vague and unspecified criteria. However, it is unclear after the panel's decision in *China – Raw Materials* whether export license criteria that is sufficiently specific for the purposes of constitutional due process necessarily avoids creating the limiting effect of uncertainty for exporters hoping to obtain a license.

Furthermore, an export licensing system can have a limiting effect in other ways besides creating uncertainty about the likelihood that a license will be granted. In at least one case, *Japan – SemiConductors*,[33] a GATT panel held that a lengthy license approval process also has a limiting effect on exportation in violation of Article XI:1. In that case, the panel held that three-month delays in an agency's export licensing process restrained exports even though the delays did not result from any "mandatory" law, regulation, or requirement.[34] Japan had required exporters to obtain licenses before exporting certain quantities of semi-conductors, and, after several years, lowered the threshold level of semi-conductors that could be shipped without a license.[35] As a result of this change in policy, the number of license applications almost doubled. The licensing agency found itself unprepared for the sudden increase of applications, and, due to the back-up, applications often could not be processed for several months.[36] The panel held that the practices resulting in the three-month delays in licensing had a limiting effect on exportation and were, therefore, *de facto* quantitative restrictions prohibited by Article XI:1.[37] It is possible that the combination of new budgetary restrictions and the imposition of an export licensing system could cause very similar delays in the licensing process to the ones deemed inconsistent with Article XI in *Japan – Semi-Conductors*.

Article XIII

In addition to violating Article XI, e-waste export restrictions may also violate Article XIII of the GATT. Article XIII prescribes rules on the administration of quantitative restrictions. Specifically, it requires Members to administer quantitative restrictions that are otherwise authorized under the GATT—which a measure would be if it was, for example, justified under

Article XX of the GATT—in a non-discriminatory manner. A WTO panel would strike down an export ban or licensing system under Article XIII if it does not conform with the principle, discussed in the following paragraphs, of most favored nation treatment.[38] However, in the name of judicial economy, WTO panels that identify violations of Article XI:1 that are not justified by Article XX generally decline to examine the measure's consistency with Article XIII.[39]

Article I

Article I, also known as the general "most favored nation" (MFN) provision, states that "any advantage, favor, privilege or immunity granted by a [WTO Member] to any product originating in or destined for any other country shall be accorded immediately and unconditionally to the like product originating in or destined for the territories of all other [WTO Members]."[40]

Unlike Article XI, which applies to any government action, Article I of the GATT applies only to specified categories of government measures, including "all rules and formalities in connection with importation and exportation."[41] This is, however, a broad category.[42] WTO panels have interpreted the phrase "in connection with importation" to encompass measures that both directly relate to the process of importation and those that might only have an impact on importation.[43] Moreover, the panel in U.S. – Poultry held that a prerequisite for importation is a rule or formality in connection with importation under Article I:1.[44] This suggests that a measure that imposes a prerequisite—licensing—on exportation must accord MFN treatment to goods from WTO Members.

A measure covered by Article I:1 violates the MFN principle if it:

1. confers *any* trade "advantage;"
2. affects "like" products; and
3. fails to accord that advantage "immediately and unconditionally" to those products.[45]

The term "advantage" in Article I:1 has been given a very broad definition to encompass any more favorable competitive opportunity or commercial status relative to those of like products destined to different WTO Members.[46] It can include, for example, variations in both the procedural and administrative requirements for imports.[47] As a result, variations in the licensing requirements for imports can constitute an advantage under Article I:1.[48] In *EC – Bananas III*,[49] for example, a WTO panel ruled that the European Union had accorded an origin-discriminatory advantage to the products of some WTO Members by imposing additional licensing requirements on imports from other WTO Members.[50] Notably, a measure may be deemed to accord an advantage even if it is written in origin neutral terms.[51]

Similarly, two products may be deemed "like" under Article I:1 even if they are subject to different tariff classifications or, for other reasons, are not exact duplicates.[52] WTO panels and the Appellate Body assess the "likeness" of two products by examining their characteristics, their end-uses, their tariff classification, and consumers' tastes and habits.[53] Where a complaining Member demonstrates that the difference in treatment between imported products is based exclusively on the products' different origins, a WTO panel will presume that there can or will be discrimination between imported products that are "like."[54]Although it is often difficult in other cases to predict whether a given measure would affect "like" products from WTO Members, a measure that affects a broad range of products may be likely to result in discrimination between at least some "like" imports.

Once a measure is found to have conferred a trade advantage that affects "like" products,[55] that measure will be deemed inconsistent with Article I:1 if it fails to accord the advantage "unconditionally." WTO panels have adopted different interpretations of the term "unconditionally,"[56] but their decisions suggest that conditions may be attached to an advantage only if they do not discriminate, either on their face or as applied, between "like" products on the basis of their countries of origin or destination.[57] For example, an advantage is not accorded "unconditionally" if some countries have to do or pay something to receive it.[58] Similarly, an advantage is not accorded "unconditionally" if some countries have to take a particular action, such as adopt a specified policy, for exports to their territories to become eligible to receive it.[59]

Notably, a measure framed in origin neutral terms so as to appear facially consistent with Article I:1 violates the MFN principle if it has a discriminatory impact on imports of like products from some WTO Members relative to others.[60] In *Canada – Autos*,[61] for example, a WTO panel examined a Canadian measure that exempted car imports from a customs duty if their manufacturers satisfied certain requirements, including establishment in Canada and the use of Canadian materials in production.[62] The panel found that the duty exemption was an "advantage" and that, although the exemption was origin neutral on its face, the structure and characteristics of the global automotive industry meant that the criteria for the exemption created origin-based discrimination among auto imports from WTO Members.[63] The panel buttressed this finding with the measure's legislative history, which suggested that the exemption was part of a scheme intended to rationalize production in the *North American* automotive market and encourage *U.S.- owned* car manufacturers to expand their production operations to Canada.[64] In other words, the panel ruled that Canada's import duty exemption was a *de facto* violation of Article I:1 because it was designed to benefit auto imports from particular sources, namely those in the United States and North America, and had the discriminatory effect it intended.[65]

Similarly, in *Indonesia – Autos*,[66] a WTO panel found that an Indonesian measure exempting certain cars from import duties and sales taxes was also inconsistent with Article I:1. In that case, an import's eligibility for the exemptions depended on facially origin neutral factors, such as the domestic car company's relationship with the foreign importer, the use of local content, and the use of the imported car parts in the assembly in Indonesia of a domestic car.[67] While these criteria, like those in *Canada – Autos*, were framed in origin neutral terms, the panel found that in practice only car imports from Korea could satisfy them.[68] Therefore, the panel ruled that the tax advantages, as applied, were accorded in a fashion that discriminated against products from WTO Members on the basis of their origin.[69]

Article XX

If a measure is found to violate a GATT obligation, a Member may seek to justify it in a WTO dispute by invoking one of the general exceptions set out in Article XX of the GATT. The defending Member has the burden, at that point, of proving that the measure both fits under one of the exceptions listed in paragraphs (a) to (j) under Article XX and satisfies the requirements imposed by Article XX's opening clauses, which form its "chapeau."[70]

Arguably, Article XX(b) may be the most viable provisional defense of a measure restricting e-waste exports. Article XX(b) justifies GATT-inconsistent measures "necessary to protect human, animal, or plant life or health." However, relative to the other Article XX sub-paragraphs, Article XX(b) imposes a high standard—"necessity"—for provisional justification. It is also possible that paragraph (g) of Article XX could be used to justify export restrictions on e-waste. Article XX(g) authorizes the imposition of GATT-inconsistent measures "relating to the conservation of exhaustible natural resources *if* such measures are made effective in conjunction with restrictions on domestic production or consumption."[71] While it may be easier for a measure to "relate" to conservation under Article XX(g) than for it to be "necessary" to protect human, animal, or plant life or health under Article XX(b), Article XX(g) only applies to export restrictions when they operate jointly with domestic restrictions.[72]

Extraterritorial Application of Article XX

Regardless of which Article XX sub-paragraph is most applicable, there is the possibility that neither is appropriate for defending e-waste export restrictions if the objective of the restrictions is to protect or conserve natural resources that are permanently inside another Member's territory. Neither Article XX(b) nor Article XX(d) state whether the objects of protection or conservation must be located in the territory of the Member imposing the challenged measure, however, in an unadopted report, a GATT panel held in *Tuna II* that policies aimed at the protection and conservation of animals—dolphins—outside of the territory of the defending Member can fall within the range of policies covered by Article XX(b).[73] No case since the establishment of the WTO has presented a panel with an opportunity to affirm, narrow, or reject the GATT panel's reasoning. Accordingly, if the GATT consistency of e-waste export restrictions reached a WTO panel, a jurisdictional issue could arise over Article XX applicability to a measure that purports to protect human and environmental health in countries where e-waste is managed in a potentially hazardous fashion.

In that scenario, the panel would need to clarify Article XX(b)'s territorial reach to determine whether it is, in fact, available to provisionally justify measures necessary to achieve *extraterritorial* effects. A panel could distinguish the objectives of the e-waste export restrictions (which would presumably be aimed at preserving the lives and health of another Member's citizens and/or its soil, air, surface water, and groundwater) from the dolphins in *Tuna II*, which move both between the territories of Member countries and within the high seas.[74]

Alternatively, a panel could find that air, soil, and water are, like dolphins, natural resources that move between Members, pointing to the transboundary flow of air, water, and chemicals in the soil. A third possibility is that a panel would hold that concerns about Members applying their environmental policies extraterritorially are addressed by the Article XX chapeau, which disfavors unilateral and coercive policies, not the provisional Article XX defense.[75]

Article XX(b)

Article XX(b) states that it may be invoked for measures "necessary to protect human, animal or plant life or health." For a Member to make a *prima facie* case that a measure restricting e-waste exports is provisionally justified under XX(b) it must show that (1) the measure's policy objective is the protection of human life or health; and (2) the measure is necessary to achieve this end. Presumably, the objective of such a measure is the protection of the life and health of the people who come into contact with the chemicals and gases released through e-waste recycling and disposal, but a panel would examine whether the measure's substance, design, architecture, and structure support this assumption.[76]

Satisfying the second element of the test under Article XX(b)—necessity—is often more problematic. WTO panels begin the necessity analysis by balancing "the relevant factors, particularly the importance of the interests or values at stake, the extent of the contribution to the achievement of the measure's objective, and its trade restrictiveness."[77] In general, the more vital or important the value being pursued, the more likely it is that the measure will be deemed necessary to achieve the desired level of protection.[78] A "necessary" measure need not be indispensable, but it must be "apt to produce a material contribution to the achievement of its objective." [79] In other words, a measure providing only a "marginal or insignificant" contribution is not "necessary" to achieve its goal.[80] In addition, the required size of the contribution is often larger for measures, such as import or export bans, that are particularly trade restrictive.[81] As a result, a panel considering the application of Article XX(b) to an e-waste export ban may require the United States to establish that the ban takes a particularly substantial step towards realizing its public health objective.[82]

If a Member makes a *prima facie* case that its measure is "necessary," this initial finding may ultimately be rejected if the panel finds that a less trade restrictive alternative was "reasonably available." [83] To qualify as a reasonably available alternative, a policy must, first, be a "genuine" alternative—that is, it must be WTO-consistent and make an equivalent contribution to the achievement of the challenged measure's objective.[84] Second, the alternative policy must be feasible and not unduly burdensome for the defending Member.[85] Alternative policies that are merely "theoretical" or would impose prohibitive costs or substantial technical difficulties on the responding Member are not reasonably available alternatives.[86]

Possible alternative policies to measures restricting e-waste exports could be, *inter alia*: increased investments in e-waste recycling infrastructure;

policies stimulating greater domestic demand for e-waste; e-waste production restrictions; and the negotiation or participation in international agreements that govern trade in e-waste.[87] If these alternative policies were identified before a WTO panel, the burden would shift to the defending Member to show that these policies would not be either equally effective at realizing the objectives of the challenged export restrictions or "reasonably available" due to their feasibility, cost, or technical requirements.

Article XX(g)

Article XX(g) provisionally justifies GATT-inconsistent measures "relating to the conservation of exhaustible natural resources *if* such measures are made effective in conjunction with restrictions on domestic production or consumption."[88] Article XX(g)'s "relating to" standard is easier for a measure to satisfy than the "necessity" standard required under Article XX(b), but Article XX(g) only applies to export restrictions when they operate jointly with domestic restrictions.[89]

A measure "relating to" the conservation of an "exhaustible natural resource" is a measure "primarily aimed" at the conservation of a natural resource, either living or non-living.[90] A measure generally meets this test if it is not overly broad—that is, if its general structure and design have a "close and genuine relationship" with the asserted policy goal.[91] In addition, to fit under Article XX(g), an export restraining measure must be "made effective in conjunction" with measures that restrain domestic production or consumption. The Appellate Body has interpreted this language as requiring "evenhandedness" in the imposition of restrictions on goods in international trade and domestic products.[92] A measure's export restraints, in other words, must coexist with domestic restrictions affecting the same good, and, although these two sets of restrictions need not be identical in form or effect, the burdens they impose on exports and domestic goods respectively should be comparable.[93] This jurisprudence illustrates that a GATT inconsistent measure related to conservation is not justified under Article XX(g) without the concurrent operation of restrictions on domestic production or consumption.[94]

Article XX Chapeau

If a measure is provisionally justified under Article XX(b) or Article XX(g), it must also satisfy the Article XX chapeau, which is generally viewed as a more difficult task.[95] The chapeau states that a measure covered by Article XX must be neither "a disguised restriction on international trade" nor "applied in a manner which would constitute a means of arbitrary or unjustifiable discrimination between countries where the same conditions prevail."[96] The chapeau strikes a balance between Article XX's two purposes: the protection of Members' sovereign authority to pursue certain policy goals and the protection of Members' rights under the GATT's substantive provisions.[97] A measure's consistency with the Article XX chapeau is, therefore, highly fact dependent .[98] Ultimately, a measure satisfies the chapeau only if (1) it is not a "disguised restriction" on trade; and (2) there is "a legitimate cause or rationale in light of the [Article XX] objectives" for the discrimination it causes.[99]

Relatively few panel or Appellate Body reports have articulated the standards for determining that a measure is a disguised restriction on international trade. Ostensibly, this analysis involves a heightened analysis of the intent behind the measure's application to discern whether the defending Member's true motive was protectionism. [100] Because the intent behind a measure "may not be easily ascertained," panels may scrutinize the "design, architecture, and revealing structure" for signs of knowing or willful "protective application."[101] A WTO panel may also consider the extent to which the measure's application has a discriminatory effect, such as benefiting a domestic industry to the detriment of a foreign one.[102] Given the rudimentary nature of WTO jurisprudence in this area, it can be difficult to predict whether a given measure would be indefensible under Article XX because its application constituted a disguised restriction on trade.

In contrast to the jurisprudence on "disguised restrictions," a host of WTO panels and Appellate Body reports have declared measures inconsistent with the Article XX chapeau because their application constituted arbitrary or unjustifiable discrimination. These decisions express a strong preference for measures applied after international negotiations or pursuant to an international agreement.[103] The seeming corollary of this preference, moreover, is the distaste that panels and the Appellate Body have shown for measures with a unilateral or coercive character.[104] As discussed below, these preferences are expressed both in the Appellate Body's interpretation of the term "discrimination" and its interpretation of the phrase "arbitrary or unjustifiable."

According to the Appellate Body, "discrimination," for the purposes of the Article XX chapeau, occurs when a measure is applied without regard for the similarity of—or differences between— the conditions in either the importing and exporting countries or two importing countries.[105] In other words, both the differential treatment of countries in which the same conditions prevail and the uniform treatment of countries where *different* conditions prevail constitute discrimination.[106] Once a measure's application is deemed discriminatory, a WTO panel will assess the nature of the discrimination to determine whether it is "arbitrary or unjustifiable." This analysis depends on whether the discrimination has "a legitimate cause or rationale in light of the [Article XX] objectives,"[107] and often requires an assessment of the actions, if any, that the defending Member took to *prevent* foreseeable discrimination.[108] As a result, a measure's discriminatory application may be "unjustifiable" if the defending Member failed to undertake "serious, good faith efforts" to engage in international negotiations to prevent discrimination.

In *U.S. – Gasoline*,[109] for example, the Appellate Body found that a regulation prescribing the methods for measuring compliance with the Clean Air Act's gasoline standards did not satisfy the requirements of the Article XX chapeau. The "Gasoline Rule" required the EPA to measure foreign refiners' compliance with these standards against a single statutory baseline even though U.S. firms' compliance could be measured via more favorable individual baselines. The Appellate Body found that the measure was applied in a discriminatory manner because the rule was not adopted or applied with regard to the costs and feasibility of compliance for foreign refiners.[110] Furthermore, the Appellate Body ruled that the Gasoline Rule was "arbitrary or unjustifiable" because the United States had failed to adequately explore international cooperation as a means of achieving the measure's objective even though its discriminatory application "must have been foreseen."[111] *U.S. – Gasoline* therefore suggests that when a measure's discriminatory application can be foreseen but might have been avoided through international cooperation, the failure to pursue that cooperation necessarily renders the cause or rationale for the discrimination illegitimate and the measure's application "arbitrary or unjustifiable discrimination."

The Appellate Body seemed to confirm this conclusion in *U.S. – Shrimp*.[112] In that case, the measure in question prohibited the importation of shrimp from countries not certified by the United States as maintaining a regulatory program or fishing environment that satisfied the U.S. standards for sea turtle protection.[113] First, the Appellate Body found that the shrimp import ban created discrimination because it was "coercive"—it effectively required other Members to adopt the same sea turtle-protection policies as the United States regardless of the different conditions in the territories of those Members.[114] The Appellate Body suggested the Department of State should have incorporated an "inquiry into the appropriateness of the regulatory program for the conditions prevailing in those exporting countries" into its implementation of the ban.[115] The Appellate Body then assessed whether this discrimination was "arbitrary or unjustifiable," writing that its approach to this question was "heavily" influenced by the U.S. failure to engage all shrimp exporting Members in negotiations before enforcing the ban.[116] Indeed, the Appellate Body ultimately found that the discrimination was unjustifiable because (1) the import ban reflected U.S. negotiations with some, but not all, WTO Members that export shrimp;[117] and (2) the United States had not even *attempted* to use existing international mechanisms to achieve international cooperation.[118] As a result, the Appellate Body wrote, the ban had a "unilateral character" that heightened both its discriminatory nature and its "unjustifiability."[119]

The Appellate Body's reasoning in *U.S. – Shrimp* was only mildly tempered by its subsequent decision in *U.S. – Shrimp (Article 21.5)*[120] that the Article XX chapeau did not require the United States to actually *conclude* international agreements with shrimp exporting countries so much as engage in "serious, good faith efforts" to *negotiate* agreements.[121] In that case, Malaysia challenged the adequacy of the measures the United States imposed to implement the Appellate Body's decision in *U.S. – Shrimp*. Specifically, the Department of State had revised its guidelines so that countries could be certified for shrimp imports once they demonstrated either that their shrimp fishing environments did not pose a threat of incidental sea turtle capture or that they had implemented, and were enforcing, a "comparably effective" regulatory program.[122] In determining whether a country's regulatory program was "comparably effective" to U.S. standards, the guidelines stated that the Department of State would "take fully into account any demonstrated differences between the shrimp fishing conditions in the United States and those in other nations."[123] In addition, the United States commenced international negotiations with Malaysia, the complaining Member, as well as other countries. Although these negotiations did not yield an agreement between the United States and Malaysia, the discrimination caused by the U.S. embargo and shrimp import certification procedures was not "arbitrary or unjustifiable" because the United States had undertaken "serious, good faith efforts" to avoid it.[124]

In sum, for a measure regulating e-waste to be justified in imposing burdens on some importing countries that it does not impose on others with the same conditions, Article XX requires some legitimate reason for the resulting discrimination. Moreover, no such legitimate reason is likely to exist if the measure was implemented as a substitute for "serious, good faith efforts" at international diplomacy with the countries most burdened by its implementation. In the e-waste context, therefore, a WTO panel could require a Member to repeal or modify a measure restricting e-waste exports in a discriminatory fashion unless the Member engaged in the Basel Convention or in serious international negotiations with the e-waste importing countries affected.

CONCLUSION

There is concern that electronic waste (e-waste) producers in the United States are opting to export e-waste containing hazardous materials to developing countries rather than disposing of the waste in the United States. E-waste is one type of hazardous waste, and, as such, its trade is regulated under a series of international agreements. The United States is a party to several agreements restricting hazardous waste trade, but it is not a party to the largest multilateral agreement in this field: the Basel Convention.

The Basel Convention forbids parties from exporting hazardous wastes to any other party who has not received notice of, and consented to, that export. It also requires parties to adopt domestic policies aimed at reducing the production of hazardous waste. Basel Convention parties have adopted an amendment to impose an absolute ban on hazardous waste export from "Annex VII" parties—members of the OECD, European Union, and Liechtenstein—to other Convention parties, which are primarily developing countries. Although some parties implemented the ban domestically, the "Ban Amendment" has not entered into force and is not expected to do so for several years.

Despite an international movement to regulate the transboundary flow of e-waste, a country that imposes restrictions on e-waste exports unilaterally may risk repercussions in the WTO system. Specifically, these restrictions may be deemed inconsistent with Articles XI:1, XIII:1, and I:1 of the GATT. Article XI:1 prohibits any government actions that impose, or result in, bans or other quantitative restrictions on exports and imports destined to WTO Members. Duties, taxes, and other charges are the only Article XI:1 consistent methods of restricting imports or exports. Article I:1 prohibits any rule or formality affecting exportation from conferring a trade "advantage"—such as exemption from export licensing requirements—to exports destined to particular countries unless it "immediately and unconditionally" confers that same advantage to "like" products destined to all other WTO Members.

Nevertheless, a WTO panel will uphold export restrictions that are inconsistent with Articles XI:1, XIII:1, and/or I:1 of the GATT if they fit under one of the exceptions listed in paragraphs (a) to (j) of Article XX and satisfy the requirements imposed by the Article XX chapeau. There are several aspects of export restrictions that may make them difficult to provisionally justify under one of Article XX's sub-paragraphs and characterize as consistent with the Article XX chapeau. For example, if e-waste export restrictions are imposed as a substitute for international diplomacy, it may be difficult to show that they are "necessary" to protect human life or health under Article XX(b). Although Article XX(g) can be used to justify measures that fail Article XX(b)'s "necessity" test, it cannot justify e-waste export restrictions imposed instead of, or otherwise without, comparable restrictions on domestic consumption or production.

Ultimately, if a WTO Member imposed e-waste export restrictions that a WTO panel or the Appellate Body deemed inconsistent with the GATT, the Member would be expected to lift or modify those restrictions. If the Member failed to do so, it could face WTO-authorized trade sanctions from the complaining Member or Members.

End Notes

[1] For a comprehensive overview of e-waste management in the United States and the harms associated with it overseas, see CRS Report R40850, *Managing Electronic Waste: Issues with Exporting E-Waste*, by Linda Luther.

[2] ENVIRONMENTAL PROTECTION AGENCY, INTERNATIONAL TRADE IN HAZARDOUS WASTE: AN OVERVIEW (November 1998), http://www.epa.gov/compliance/resources/policies/civil/rcra/intnltrahazwas-rpt.pdf.

[3] OECD Council Decision on the Control of Transboundary Movements of Wastes Destined for Recovery Operations, March 30, 1992, T.I.A.S. No. 11880; Agreement Concerning the Transboundary Movement of Hazardous Waste, U.S.- Can., October 28, 1986, T.I.A.S. No. 11099 (entered into force November 8, 1986); Agreement of Cooperation Regarding the Transboundary Shipments of Hazardous Wastes and Hazardous Substances, U.S.-Mex., November 12, 1986, T.I.A.S. No. 11269 (entered into force January 29, 1987). The United States is also a party to two bilateral agreements with Malaysia and Costa Rica, both of which govern the export of hazardous waste from those countries into the United States. Agreement Concerning the Transboundary Movement of Hazardous Waste, U.S.-Malay., March 10, 1995, T.I.A.S. No. 12612; Agreement Concerning the Transboundary Movement of Hazardous Wastes from Costa Rica to the United States, U.S.-Costa Rica, November 17, 1997.

[4] March 22, 1989, KAV 2634 (entered into force May 5, 1992), *available at* http://basel.int/text/17Jun2010-conv-e.pdf. For more information on the Basel Convention, visit http://basel.int/index.html. Notably, in the 1990s, the United States took some steps towards becoming a party to the Convention: it signed the Convention on March 3, 1990 and the U.S. Senate provided its advice and consent to ratification in 1992. 138 CONG. REC. 22,860-61 (August 11, 1992). For information on the procedures a country must follow in

order to become a party to the Convention, see http://www.basel.int/ Procedures /BecomingaParty/tabid/1280/Default.aspx.

[5] A list of parties and the status of ratifications is available here: http://www.basel.int/ Countries/ StatusofRatifications/ PartiesSignatories/tabid/1290/Default.aspx.

[6] Decision III/1 Amendment to the Basel Convention (Third meeting of the Conference of the Parties) (1995), *available at* http://basel.int/meetings/cop/cop1-4/cop3decisions_e.pdf.

[7] SECRETARIAT OF THE BASEL CONVENTION, THE BASEL CONVENTION BAN AMENDMENT, http://basel.int/pub/ baselban.html; Daniel Pruzin, *Basel Convention Will Consider Plan to Ban Hazardous Waste Shipments*, DAILY REPORT FOR EXECUTIVES (October 6, 2011). Under the so-called CLI decision (the Country Led Initiative to Improve the Effectiveness of the Basel Convention), the Ban Amendment will enter into force once it is ratified by three-fourths of the parties that were Convention parties at the time of the Amendment's adoption. SECRETARIAT OF THE BASEL CONVENTION, HISTORIC AGREEMENT ENDS 15 YEAR DEADLOCK OVER BANNING NORTH-SOUTH MOVEMENTS OF HAZARDOUS WASTE (October 25, 2011); Daniel Pruzin, *Basel Convention Agrees on Implementation of Proposed Hazardous Waste Shipment Ban*, DAILY REPORT FOR EXECUTIVES (October 24, 2011). As of January 2012, 17 more ratifications were reportedly required for the Ban Amendment to take effect. Daniel Pruzin, *Hazardous Waste Shipment Restrictions, Reorganization Top Treaty Agendas*, DAILY REPORT FOR EXECUTIVES (January 13, 2012). The CLI decision also established a framework under which countries who wish to participate in the international waste trade could take steps to minimize its health and environmental impacts. The text of the CLI proposal is available at http://archive.basel.int/meetings/cop/cop10/documents/05e.pdf.

[8] There are over 150 countries in the World Trade Organization. For an up to date list, see http://www.wto.org/english/ thewto_e/whatis_e/tif_e/org6_e.htm.

[9] For a more detailed overview of the WTO dispute settlement process, see CRS Report RS20088, *Dispute Settlement in the World Trade Organization (WTO): An Overview*, by Jeanne J. Grimmett.

[10] *See* PETER VAN DEN BOSSCHE, THE LAW AND POLICY OF THE WORLD TRADE ORGANIZATION 448 (2d ed. 2008). For example, in *Japan – Semiconductors*, a GATT panel found that export licensing practices leading to delays of up to three months in the issuing of licenses for semi-conductors were inconsistent with Article XI:1. Report of the Panel, *Japan – Trade in Semi-Conductors* (May 4, 1988) GATT B.I.S.D. (35th Supp.), 31 at 118.

[11] *See* Van Den Bossche, *supra* footnote 10, at 448-49. Measures that, as applied, discourage and reduce exports of a particular product constitute *de facto* quantitative prohibition and are also inconsistent with Article XI:1 of the GATT. *See* Panel Report, *Argentina – Measures Affecting the Export of Bovine Hides and the Import of Finished Leather*, paras. 11.17, 11.20-11.21, WT/DS155/R (December 19, 2000). In one case to consider the *de facto* consistency of a measure affecting exports, *Argentina – Bovine Hides*, the WTO panel ultimately found that the complainant had failed to allege sufficient facts to prove "clearly and convincingly" that the measures at issue caused the "unusually low" levels of exports of hides. *Id.* at 11.50. However, more recently, in *Brazil – Tyres*, a measure imposing fines on the marketing, transportation, and, *inter alia*, storage of imported retreaded tires was found to have "the effect of" penalizing the act of importing these tires, and, therefore, deemed inconsistent with Article XI:1. Panel Report, *Brazil – Measures Affecting Imports of Used Tyres*, ¶ 7.372, WT/DS332/R (June 12, 2007).

[12] *See* Report of the Panel, *EC – Payments and Subsidies Paid to Processors and Producers of Oilseeds* (January 25, 1990) GATT B.I.S.D. (37th Supp.), 36 at ¶ 150 ("An import quota constitutes an import restriction within the meaning of Article XI:1 whether or not it actually impeded imports.").

[13] *See id. See also* Panel Report, *Colombia – Indicative Prices and Restrictions on Ports of Entry*, paras. 7.326 -7.330, WT/DS366/R (April 27, 2009) (indicating that a Member has standing to enforce a provision of the GATT even if the measure being challenged does not, at the time the dispute is heard, restrict existing trade flows between the complaining and defending Members).

[14] *See* Report of the Panel, *Japan – Trade in Semi-Conductors, supra* footnote 10, at ¶ 118 ("The standard applicable to import licenses should, by analogy, be applied also to export licenses ... "); Wen-Chen Shih, *Energy Security, GATT/WTO, and Regional Agreements*, 49 NAT. RES. J. 433, 451 (2009) (stating that there are indications that "the jurisprudence concerning quantitative restrictions on import in the interpretation and application of Article XI:1 also applies to exports.").

[15] Panel Report, *Brazil – Measures Affecting Imports of Retreaded Tyres*, WT/DS332/R (June 12, 2007).

[16] *See id.* at paras. 2.8, 7.7. Often referred to as a "trade bloc," MERCOSUR, or the Common Market of the South, is a cooperative economic and political framework established by Brazil, Argentina, Uruguay, and Paraguay. For more background on MERCOSUR, see CRS Report RL33620, *Mercosur: Evolution and Implications for U.S. Trade Policy*, by J. F. Hornbeck.

[17] *Id.* at 7.14.

[18] Panel Report, *India – Quantitative Restrictions on Imports of Agricultural, Textile and Industrial Products*, WT/DS90/R (April 6, 1999).

[19] *Id.* at paras. 5.139, 5.142.

[20] *Id.* at 5.142.

[21] *Id.* The panel wrote that this precluded the distribution of the affected imports to consumers unable to import the products for direct use. *Id.*

[22] See Panel Report, Brazil – Tyres, supra footnote 15, at 7.371 (quoting Panel Report, India – Measures Affecting the Automotive Sector, ¶ 7.265, WT/DS146/R (December 21, 2001)). See e.g., Panel Report, China – Measures Related to the Exportation of Various Raw Materials, 7.894, WT/DS394/R (July 5, 2011); Panel Report, Colombia – Ports of Entry, supra footnote 13, at 7.240; Panel Report, India – Quantitative Restrictions, supra footnote 18, at 3.11; Panel Report, Argentina – Bovine Hides, supra footnote 11, at 11.33 (describing a quantitative restriction as a measure having an "inherent 'chilling effect' on the exporter").

[23] Panel Report, *Colombia – Ports of Entry, supra* footnote 13, at 7.240.

[24] *See, e.g.,* Panel Report, *India – Quantitative Restrictions, supra* footnote 18, at paras. 5.129, 5.130.

[25] *See, e.g.,* Panel Report, *China – Raw Materials, supra* footnote 22, at 7.917.

[26] Panel Report, China – Measures Related to the Exportation of Various Raw Materials, WT/DS394/R (July 5, 2011).

[27] Id. at paras. 7.902, 7.917.

[28] See id. at 7.921.

[29] Id. at paras. 7.945, 7.946.

[30] Id.

[31] Panel Report, China – Raw Materials, supra footnote 26, at 7.921. "The possibility to deny the license" would, in this scenario, be "ever present" because "the conditions for granting it are subject to the demands of the particular licensing authority." Id. at paras. 7.921, 7.948.

[32] Id. at 7.948.

[33] Report of the Panel, Japan – Trade in Semi-Conductors (May 4, 1988) GATT B.I.S.D. (35th Supp.), 31.

[34] Id. at paras. 108-109, 118.

[35] Id. at 22.

[36] Id.

[37] See Id. at 118.

[38] Under Article XIII:1, WTO Members may not apply quantitative import prohibitions or restrictions unless the importation of like products of all third countries is similarly prohibited or restricted. GATT, Art. XIII:1.

[39] E.g., Report of the Panel, India – Quantitative Restrictions, supra footnote 18, at 5.17; Panel Report, U.S. – Import Prohibition of Certain Shrimp and Shrimp Products, 7.22, WT/DS58/R (May 15, 1998).

[40] GATT, Art. I:1.

[41] The other specified categories of government measures are: "customs duties and charges of any kind imposed on or in connection with importation or exportation or imposed on the international transfer of payments for imports or exports, and with respect to the method of levying such duties and charges... and with respect to all matters referred to in paragraphs 2 and 4 of Article III." GATT, Art. I:1. For reference, Article III:2 of the GATT covers internal taxes or other internal charges, and Article III:4 governs all laws, regulations, and requirements affecting the internal sale, offering for sale, purchase, transportation, distribution, or use of a product.

[42] Panel Report, *U.S. – Certain Measures Affecting Imports of Poultry from China*, 7.407, WT/DS392/R (September 23, 2010).

[43] *Id.* at ¶ 7.410 (citing Panel Report, *India – Measures Affecting the Automotive Sectors*, 7.257, WT/DS146/R (December 21, 2001)).

[44] *Id.* at paras. 7.409 – 7.410.

[45] Panel Report, *Indonesia – Certain Measures Affecting the Automobile Industry*, WT/DS54/R, 14.138 (July 2, 1998).

[46] Panel Report, *EC – Regime for the Importation, Sale, and Distribution of Bananas*, WT/DS27/R/GTM, 7.239 (May 22, 1997); Panel Report, *Colombia – Ports of Entry, supra* footnote 13, at ¶ 7.341. In *Colombia – Ports of Entry*, the panel wrote that a measure also gives rise to an Article I:1 "advantage" when it gives an operator the opportunity to "choose how to operate his business in order to enhance his profitability and competitiveness." *Id.* at 7.351.

[47] *See* Report of the Panel, *EC – Regime for the Importation, Sale, and Distribution of Bananas*, WT/DS27/R/USA, paras. 7.193, 7.194 (May 22, 1997).

[48] *See id.* In *EC – Bananas III*, the Appellate Body affirmed a WTO panel report ruling that the European Union's import licensing procedures for bananas were inconsistent with Article I:1 of the GATT because they imposed heightened requirements for banana importers from some WTO Members but not all. Appellate Body Report, *EC – Regime for the Importation, Sale, and Distribution of Bananas*, 206, WT/DS27/AB/R (September 9, 1997).

[49] Panel Report, *EC – Regime for the Importation, Sale, and Distribution of Bananas*, WT/DS27/R/USA (May 22, 1997).

[50] *Id.* at paras. 7.193, 7.194.

[51] *See* Panel Report, *Canada – Certain Measures Affecting the Automotive Industry*, paras. 14.123, 14.147, 15.1(c), WT/DS139/R (February 11, 2000).

[52] Rex J. Zedalis, *A Theory of GATT Like Product Common Language Cases*, 27 VAND. J. TRANSNAT'L L. 33, 78-84 (1994). *See* MICHAEL TREBILOCK, UNDERSTANDING

TRADE LAW 40-41 (2011). For example, whether a person could obtain a license to export a used iPad would depend on its intended end-use—that is, whether the iPad was being exported for reuse, as result of a recall, pursuant to a warranty, or for recycling. It is possible that a WTO panel would find that these are not "like" products because their end-uses are different, and, therefore, that a measure discriminating between them does not violate Article I. It may be more likely, however, that a WTO panel would find that the two used iPads *are* "like" products because they have the exact same product characteristics, share the same tariff classification, and are not distinguished from one another by their consumers.

[53] Van den Bossche, *supra* footnote 10, at 330-31. *See* Report of the Panel, *U.S. – Poultry*, *supra* footnote 42, at 7.425.

[54] Report of the Panel, *U.S. – Poultry*, *supra* footnote 42, at paras. 7.427, 7.428; Report of the Panel, *Colombia – Ports of Entry*, *supra* footnote 13, at paras. 7.356, 7.357.

[55] For a definition of "like" products, see *supra* footnote 52.

[56] *Compare* Panel Report, *Canada – Autos*, *supra* footnote 51, at paras. 10.23-10.25 (finding that measures are inconsistent with Article I:1 "not because they involve the application of conditions that were not related to the imported product but because they involve conditions that entailed different treatment of imported products upon their origin") *and* Panel Report, *Colombia – Ports of Entry*, *supra* footnote 13, at 7.362 ("In line with the approach elaborated in the *Canada – Autos* dispute, the Panel considers that it may thus assess whether the advantage is conferred 'immediately and unconditionally' based on whether an advantage... is not similarly accorded to those products originating in Panama for reasons related to [their] origin or the conduct of Panama.") *with* Panel Report, *EC – Condition's for the Granting of Tariff Preferences*, ¶ 7.59, WT/DS246/R (December 1, 2003) (writing that the term "unconditionally" in Article I:1 retains its "ordinary" meaning: "not limited by or subject to any conditions").

[57] *See* Panel Report, *Colombia – Ports of Entry*, *supra* footnote 13, at paras. 7.362- 7.366; Charles Benoit, *Picking Tariff Winners: Non-Product Related PPMS and DSB Interpretations of "Unconditionally" Within Article I:1*, 42 GEO. J. INT'L L. 583, 600 (2011) (writing that the panel decisions "favoring the flexible interpretations" of the term "unconditionally" include the latest panel report—*Colombia – Ports of Entry*—and have "contained lengthier and more in depth discussions of the meaning of Article I:1.").

[58] *See* Van den Bossche, *supra* footnote 10, at 332.

[59] *See id.*

[60] *See* Panel Report, *Canada – Autos*, *supra* footnote 51, at paras. 14.123, 14.147, 15.1(c); Trebilock, *supra* footnote 52, at 41.

[61] Panel Report, *Canada – Certain Measures Affecting the Automotive Industry*, WT/DS139/R (February 11, 2000).

[62] *Id.* at paras. 2.1, 2.2.

[63] *Id.* at paras. 10.43-10.45. In particular, the panel found that the automotive industry relies heavily on "intra-firm trade"—that is, the major automotive corporations in Canada only imported their own make of motor vehicles and those of affiliated companies. *Id.* at paras. 10.43, 10.45.

[64] Panel Report, *Canada – Autos*, *supra* footnote 61, at 10.49.

[65] *See id.*

[66] Panel Report, *Indonesia – Certain Measures Affecting the Automobile Industry*, WT/DS54/R (July 2, 1998).

[67] *Id.* at paras. 14.145-14.146.

[68] *Id.* at 14.145.

[69] *Id.*

[70] Appellate Body Report, *U.S. – Standards for Reformulated and Conventional Gasoline*, 22, WT/DS2/AB/R (April 29, 1996); Panel Report, *China – Measures Related to the Exportation of Various Raw Materials*, 7.359, WT/DS394/R (July 5, 2011).

[71] GATT, Art. XX(g) (emphasis added).

[72] Appellate Body Report, *U.S. – Gasoline*, *supra* footnote 70, at 20.

[73] Panel Report, *U.S. – Restrictions on Imports of Tuna*, paras. 5.20, 5.33, DS29/R (June 16, 1994) (unadopted).

[74] *See id.* at 5.17. The high seas are an area where Members can, to some extent, jointly exercise regulatory autonomy. *See id.*

[75] *Compare* GATT Panel Report, *U.S. – Restrictions on Imports of Tuna*, paras. 5.27, 5.32 (September 3, 1991), GATT B.I.S.D. (39th Supp.) (unadopted) (stating that if Articles XX(b) and (g) justified measures with extraterritorial objectives, each Member "could unilaterally determine" the environmental policies of other Members) *with* Appellate Body Report, *United States – Import Prohibition of Certain Shrimp and Shrimp Products*, paras. 171-172, WT/DS58/AB/R (October 12, 1998) (finding that the "unilateral character" of a U.S. environmental measure that restricted certain shrimp imports heightened both its discriminatory nature and its "unjustifiability" under the Article XX chapeau).

[76] *See* PETER VAN DEN BOSSCHE, THE LAW AND POLICY OF THE WORLD TRADE ORGANIZATION 622 (2d ed. 2008). *See, e.g.,* Panel Report, *EC – Tariff Preferences for Developing Countries*, paras. 7.180-7.210, WT/DS246/R (December 1, 2003) (finding that the policy of the challenged measure is sustainable development, not the protection of human life or health, and therefore the measure cannot be justified under Article XX(b)); Panel Report, *China – Raw Materials*, *supra* footnote 70, at paras. 7.507 - 7.512 (stating that the panel "needs persuasive evidence of a connection" between the challenged measures and their asserted environmental goals and concluding that "neither the measures implementing the export restrictions, nor the contemporaneous laws and regulations, convey in their texts that the export restrictions are contributing to, or form part of, a comprehensive program for the fulfillment of its stated environmental objective").

[77] Appellate Body Report, *Brazil – Measures Affecting Imports of Retreaded Tyres*, 178, WT/DS332/AB/R (December 3, 2007).

[78] Panel Report, *China – Raw Materials*, *supra* footnote 70, at 7.487. *See* Appellate Body Report, *Korea – Measures Affecting Imports of Fresh, Chilled and Frozen Beef*, ¶ 162, WT/DS169/AB/R (December 11, 2000).

[79] Appellate Body Report, *Brazil – Tyres*, *supra* footnote 77, at paras. 150-151.

[80] *Id.*

[81] *Id.* at ¶ 61 (stating that quantitative restrictions are "as trade –restrictive as can be"). *See* Panel Report, *China – Raw Materials*, *supra* footnote 70, at paras. 7.487 - 7.488.

[82] Appellate Body Report, *Brazil – Tyres*, *supra* footnote 77, at 210.

[83] *Id.* at ¶ 156.

[84] *Id.*

[85] *Id.*

[86] *Id.* (quoting Appellate Body Report, *U.S. – Measures Affecting the Cross-Border Supply of Gambling and Betting Services*, paras. 308, 311, WT/DS285/AB/R (April 7, 2005)).

[87] *See, e.g.,* Panel Report, *China – Raw Materials*, *supra* footnote 70, at paras. 7.578 – 7.590 (finding that increased investments in scrap recycling infrastructure, policies stimulating local demand for scrap, and production restrictions were all "reasonably available" less trade restrictive alternatives to China's export restrictions on certain raw materials). *See also* Appellate Body Report, *U.S. – Shrimp*, *supra* footnote 75, 170 (reasoning that, because the United States had signed *an*

international agreement establishing mechanisms for conserving sea turtles affected by shrimping, "consensual and multilateral procedures are available and feasible" to achieve the same objectives as the challenged measure); Appellate Body Report, *U.S. – Import Prohibition of Certain Shrimp and Shrimp Products, Recourse to Article 21.5 of the DSU by Malaysia*, 128, WT/DS58/AB/R (October 22, 2001) (stating that the Inter-American Convention was evidence that an alternative course of action based on cooperation and consensus was reasonably available).

[88] GATT, Art. XX(g) (emphasis added).

[89] Appellate Body Report, *U.S. – Gasoline*, *supra* footnote 70, at 20.

[90] *Id.* at 18; Appellate Body Report, *U.S. – Shrimp*, *supra* footnote 75, at 128.

[91] Appellate Body Report, *China – Measures Related to the Exportation of Various Raw Materials*, ¶ 355, WT/DS394/AB/R (January 30, 2012); Appellate Body Report, *U.S. – Shrimp*, *supra* footnote 75, ¶ 136; Van den Bossche, *supra* footnote 76, at 637.

[92] Appellate Body Report, *U.S. – Gasoline*, *supra* footnote 70, at 20-21; Van den Bossche, *supra* footnote 76, at 637..

[93] *See* Van den Bossche, *supra* footnote 76, at 638. However, it is unclear whether a measure that fails to accord evenhanded treatment to domestic and imported goods would be considered "primarily aimed" at conservation. *See* Appellate Body Report, *U.S. – Gasoline*, *supra* footnote 70, at 21-22.

[94] *See* Appellate Body Report, *U.S. – Gasoline*, *supra* footnote 70, at 21; Van den Bossche, *supra* footnote 76, at 638.

[95] Appellate Body Report, *U.S. – Gasoline*, *supra* footnote 70, at 22-23.

[96] GATT, Art. XX.

[97] *See* Appellate Body Report, *United States – Shrimp*, *supra* footnote 75, at paras. 158-159.

[98] *Id.*

[99] Appellate Body Report, *Brazil – Tyres*, *supra* footnote 77, at 225; Appellate Body Report, *U.S. – Gasoline*, *supra* footnote 70, at 23-24.

[100] *See* Van den Bossche, *supra* footnote 76, at 650. In addition, the term "restriction" has been construed broadly to encompass both restrictions *on* international trade and discrimination *in* international trade. *See* Panel Report, *European Communities – Measures Affecting Asbestos and Asbestos-Containing Products*, 8.235, WT/DS135/R (September 18, 2000) (citing Appellate Body Report, *U.S. – Gasoline*, *supra* footnote 70, at 25).

[101] Panel Report, *EC – Asbestos*, *supra* footnote 100, at 8.236.

[102] *See, e.g.*, *id.* at paras. 8.237 - 8.239.

[103] *See* Appellate Body Report, *United States – Shrimp (Article 21.5)*, *supra* footnote 87, at 124 ("Clearly, and 'as far as possible,' a multilateral approach is strongly preferred.") (quoting Principle 12 of the Rio Declaration on Environment and Development).

[104] Appellate Body Report, *U.S. – Shrimp*, *supra* footnote 75, at 172.

[105] *See id.*; Van den Bossche, *supra* footnote 76, at 644.

[106] Van den Bossche, *supra* footnote 76, at 644. *See* Appellate Body Report, *U.S. – Shrimp*, *supra* footnote 75, at 172.

[107] Appellate Body Report, *Brazil – Tyres*, *supra* footnote 77, at 225; Appellate Body Report, *U.S. – Gasoline*, *supra* footnote 70, at 23-24.

[108] *See, e.g.*, Appellate Body Report, *U.S. – Gasoline*, *supra* footnote 70, at 28 (stating that the United States failed to adequately export international cooperation and "the resulting discrimination must have been foreseen").

[109] Appellate Body Report, *U.S. – Standards for Reformulated and Conventional Gasoline*, WT/DS2/AB/R (April 29, 1996).

[110] *Id.* at 28.

[111] *Id.*

[112] Appellate Body Report, *United States – Import Prohibition of Certain Shrimp and Shrimp Products*, paras. 171-172, WT/DS58/AB/R (October 12, 1998).

[113] *Id.* at 161.

[114] *Id.* at paras. 161, 164.

[115] *Id.* at paras. 161, 165.

[116] *Id.* at ¶ 166 (stating that the U.S. failure to engage these WTO Members in "serious across-the-board negotiations with the objective of concluding bilateral or multilateral agreements" "bears heavily" on the analysis).

[117] *See* Appellate Body Report, *U.S. – Shrimp*, *supra* footnote 112, at 172.

[118] *See id.* at 171.

[119] *Id.* at 172.

[120] Appellate Body Report, *U.S. – Import Prohibition of Certain Shrimp and Shrimp Products, Recourse to Article 21.5 of the DSU by Malaysia*, WT/DS58/AB/R (October 22, 2001).

[121] *Id.* at ¶ 134. For a list of actions that, when taken together, qualified as "serious, good faith efforts" in this case, see paragraph 131 of that report. Ultimately, the Appellate Body found no fault with the panel's analysis that the United States should be judged on the basis of its "active participation and its financial support to the negotiations." *Id.* at paras. 132, 133.

[122] Appellate Body Report, *U.S. – Shrimp (Article 21.5)*, *supra* footnote 120, at paras. 6, 7.

[123] *Id.* at ¶ 6. *See also* Revised Guidelines for the Implementation of 609 of P.L. 101-162 Relating to the Protection of Sea Turtles, 64 Fed. Reg. 36,946 (July 8, 1999) ("In reviewing any such information, the Department of State will take fully into account any demonstrated differences between the shrimp fishing conditions in the United States and those in other nations, as well as information available from other sources.").

[124] *See* Appellate Body Report, *U.S. – Shrimp (Article 21.5)*, *supra* footnote 120, at paras. 123, 134.

INDEX

A

B

C

D

E

F

G

H

I

J

K

L

M

N

O

P

T

U

V

W

Y